CHRISTOLOGY: A GUIDE FOR THE PERPLEXED

GUIDES FOR THE PERPLEXED AVAILABLE FROM CONTINUUM

CHRISTOLOGY: A GUIDE FOR THE PERPLEXED

ALAN J. SPENCE

t&t clark

Published by T&T Clark
A Continuum imprint
The Tower Building   80 Maiden Lane, Suite 704
11 York Road   New York
London SE1 7NX   NY 10038

www.continuumbooks.com

British Library Cataloguing-in-Publication Data
A catalogue record for this book is available from the British Library

ISBN-10: HB: 0-567-03194-2
         PB: 0-567-03195-0
ISBN-13: HB: 978-0-567-03194-5
         PB: 978-0-567-03195-2

Typeset by Newgen Imaging System Pvt Ltd, Chennai, India
Printed and bound in Great by MPG Books Ltd, Bodmin, Cornwall

For
Winifred Marie

CONTENTS

LIST OF ABBREVIATIONS

ANF	*Ante-Nicene Fathers, reprinted by William B. Eerdmans (Grand Rapids, Michigan, 1985ff.)*
CD	*Church Dogmatics (Edingugh, T&T Clark, 1932–69)*
Contra Arius	*Four Discourses Against the Arians*
Dial.	*Dialogue with Trypho*
Eph.	*Epistle to the Ephesians*
NPNF	*Nicene and Post-Nicene Fathers, reprinted by William B. Eerdmans (Grand Rapids, Michigan, 1975ff.)*
Smyrn.	*Epistle to the Smyrnaens*
Trall.	*Epistle to the Trallians Works The Works of John Owen ed. by William H. Goold, reprinted by the banner of Truth Trust (London, 1965–8)*

PREFACE

To say that Jesus Christ is determinative for Christian faith appears to be doing no more than stating the obvious. The extent, however, to which the Church's conception of Jesus has shaped its understanding of God, humanity and the world, has not always been fully appreciated. All the Church's major doctrines including those of the Trinity, salvation, sanctification, creation, final judgement and the coming Kingdom of God have been influenced, if not governed, by the interpretation that Christians give to his person. This means that a comprehensive discussion of who this man really is would have to include pretty much everything that Christians distinctively hold to be true. And that is rather more material than can be included in most theological libraries let alone a book of this length.

It has, however, been the practice of the Church in its christological reflection to focus on one particular aspect of Jesus, that is, on the relation of the divine and human in him. And the concentration of its attention on this specific area has proved to be remarkably fruitful. This is because the way in which theologians interpret this relation inevitably influences almost everything else that they say about him. It provides, as it were, the DNA or basic building block for all their theological constructions. This means that as we seek to come to terms with various christological theories and ideas in the course of this book we will always have an eye to what is being stated or implied of the relation of the divine and human in the person of Jesus.

The method we have used in our study can be compared to that of a hostess who is required to introduce a late arrival to a group of distinguished guests at a dinner party. An important conversation has been going on among them for some time. In order that the newcomer can be brought up to speed and participate in the ongoing

discussion, the hostess briefly summarizes what each of the participants has said so far and so supplies an outline of the conversation's
development. For our consideration of Jesus' person we have invited
20 or so influential theologians, ancient and modern, to the party.
Their input into the christological discussion of the Church has
either been significant in itself or is representative of an influential
historical development. We have tended, particularly in the later
chapters, to choose for examination one or two of their major writings. The intention is that readers, as recent arrivals to the table,
might have the freedom, if they so wish, to go back and examine
these ideas directly without having to rely on the interpretive summary of this particular host. They can, as it were, interrogate the
invited guests for themselves at their own leisure and in this way
become active participants in the ongoing discussion.

The subject matter of the book has been divided evenly into two
principal sections: classical christology and modern christology.
These are not strictly consecutive movements. Although modern
christology originated with the emergence of Socinian ideas in the
early years of the Protestant Reformation, classical christology has
continued to serve as a parallel interpretative scheme not only within
the Orthodox and Catholic churches but also in some of the more
orthodox Protestant traditions. To continue with the analogy of the
dinner party, it is as though a number of the guests had at some time
in the evening drifted into the living room to carry on their conversation independently of the original party, sometimes breaking up into
even smaller sub-groups in response to new ideas. Why they left the
dining hall and what fresh insights they brought to the discussion are
of course matters of great interest. So is the question of whether or
not there is any possibility that the conversations might one day be
reunited or at least what the conditions might be for such a conver-
gence to take place. A consideration of this last question is the subject
matter of the concluding chapter.

I am indebted to three of my friends Lincoln Harvey, Oliver
Crisp and Susanah Ticciati, all teachers of christology in British
theological institutions, for reading the draft of the book and making numerous helpful suggestions as to how it may be improved both
in its presentation and in its theology. My thanks also go to Georgina
Brindley and Thomas Kraft of T&T Clark for inviting me to contribute to the 'Guides for the Perplexed' series.

CLASSICAL CHRISTOLOGY

CHAPTER ONE

THE PARADOX

QUESTIONS ABOUT JESUS

From their earliest days Christians have offered their worship and allegiance, not just to the one God who made the heavens and the earth, but to a Galilean preacher, who was executed while still a young man during the reign of Emperor Tiberius Caesar. Most Jews and Muslims regard such devotion to an historical person as both absurd and impious, if not blasphemous. Christians seem generally far less conscious of just how odd or paradoxical their religion looks from the outside. They exalt Jesus in their prayers, their hymns and their creeds with little awareness of how strange such action might appear.

How did such a situation ever arise? Jews and Muslims have enormous respect for their own major prophetic figures but have always been careful not to allow such esteem to develop into any suggestion that the prophet himself was worthy of divine honour. The line between what is appropriate and inappropriate reverence for such persons has been deeply drawn in their communal religious consciousness. Those who would stray across it are always in serious danger of being charged with blasphemy.[1]

Why then are Christians so unconcerned about ascribing to Jesus such exalted status? It certainly isn't a practice that they came to gradually. On the contrary, there is clear indication that after his death the first generation of believers, including a number of those who had known him personally, began to honour Jesus in their hymns, blessings, salutations and prayers with a status that other monotheists have generally found to be wholly improper for one born of a woman. It is interesting to reflect on how this curious state of affairs might have come about. It is a question that has in recent times prompted much scholarly research.

A number of studies focused on the titles that the early church used when referring to Jesus and sought to trace through them a pattern of increasing religious devotion to him, particularly in the predominantly Gentile churches, which were less inhibited by Jewish monotheistic tradition.[2] More recently, scholars have shown that a high level of divine reverence was paid to Jesus by the Jewish-Christian community almost from the start and that this is indicated in some of the earliest Christian literature. In his book *How on Earth Did Jesus Become a God?* Larry Hurtado argues persuasively that

> [o]ur earliest Christian writings, from approximately 50-60 C.E., already presuppose cultic devotion to Jesus as a familiar and defining feature of Christian circles wherever they were found (see 1Cor. 1.2).[3]

One of the most elegant of these early ascriptions of high honour to Jesus is to be found in a letter that one of his Jewish contemporaries wrote to a newly established community of Christians:
[H]ave the same attitude of mind Christ Jesus had:

> who, being in the very nature of God,
> did not consider equality with God something to be used to
> his own advantage;
> rather, he made himself nothing
> by taking the very nature of a servant,
> being made in human likeness.
> And being found in the appearance as a human being,
> He humbled himself
> by becoming obedient to death – even death on a cross!
> Therefore God exalted him to the highest place
> and gave him the name that is above every name,
> that at the name of Jesus every knee should bow,
> in heaven and earth and under the earth,
> and that every tongue acknowledge that Jesus Christ is Lord,
> to the glory of God the Father.[4]

What is particularly interesting is that most commentators believe that the poetic style of this piece of writing indicates that Paul, the author of the letter, most probably borrowed it from an earlier hymn. It is apparent that Christians offered Jesus an extraordinary level of honour from around the time the first churches came into being.

What is surprising is that while non-Christian Jews were deeply disturbed by the growing reverence paid by Christians to Jesus, such a development appears to have raised no internal controversy within the Church. There is no indication that Christians were offended by the high praise offered to him by some of their more enthusiastic fellow-believers. No righteous concern seems to have been shown that traditional Jewish monotheism was under threat from some over-exuberant Christian devotional practice. No voice was heard in the Church warning that the development of such Christian piety could undermine the authoritative words of the 'Shema':

Hear, O Israel, the Lord our God, the Lord is one. (Deut. 4.4)

Why was this? How was Christian esteem for Jesus able to move apparently unchallenged over the critical line of demarcation between creature and creator? In short, how was such a remarkable degree of consensus reached so soon within the Church on a matter which outsiders generally regarded as blasphemous? The early church did of course give serious theological thought to how it might speak about Jesus, at some transcendent level, to account for his elevated place in its faith and spirituality. This is apparent, for instance, in the claims made for the Galilean carpenter's son in the prologue of John's Gospel:

In the beginning was the Word, and the Word was with God, and the Word was God. He was with God in the beginning. Through him all things were made, without him nothing was made that was made. In him was life and that life was the light of men. . . . The Word became flesh and lived for a while among us. We have seen his glory, the glory of the one and only Son who came from the Father, full of grace and truth. (Jn 1.1,2,3,14)

But such theological reflection and insight, articulated in Christian literature towards the end of the first century, was an outcome of early Christian devotional practice rather than the actual cause of it. What was it then that brought about this tide of devotion to Jesus which so quickly overwhelmed the longstanding Jewish religious strictures forbidding the ascription of divine glory to any mortal man or woman?

The New Testament narratives bear witness to a dramatic sequence of events leading to the formation of the Church which can be summarized loosely in this way. The prophetic ministry of John the Baptist and the preaching and healing ministry of Jesus fuelled the expectation of many in Judea and Galilee that the appearance of the coming Kingdom of God was imminent. The announcement of Jesus' resurrection after he had been unjustly executed by the Romans, along with the public outpouring of the Holy Spirit on the early disciples, was a clear signal to the faithful that the promised divine Kingdom, already apparent in the signs, wonders and miracles of Jesus' ministry, was finally breaking into the present age. It was in this context that many responded positively to the apostolic proclamation of the Gospel. They were baptized for the remission of sins and through their reception of the Spirit came to know the salvation of God. The pronouncement that Jesus had been elevated to a position of authority at the right hand of God was confirmed by their own dramatic experience of the Spirit, a token for them of his present enthronement in heaven. In the context of such an interpretation of these events, it is not difficult to understand why the devotion of those early disciples should so quickly have crossed, or at least completely reinterpreted, the boundaries of monotheistic strictures.

THE TASK OF CHRISTOLOGY

Once Jesus was perceived by the believing community in this light and elevated to a position of divine status in its worship, the Church found itself facing, even as it continues to face today, a whole host of complex and baffling questions about his person. Responding to them has been the task of christology. Christology can be described as the faltering attempt of the Church to provide a coherent conceptual and theological explanation of Jesus' person, in harmony with the scriptural testimony, which is able to account for his role in its worship and faith.

Christology is, according to this description, a distinct discipline from one which seeks to show why Jesus is indeed worthy of the status that the Church ascribes to him. Its primary concern is not to persuade the agnostic that he is the promised Messiah or to marshal evidence in support of his divinity for those who are yet to be convinced. It has to do, rather, with making sense of what is already there, that is, the faith and practice of the believing community. Christology is consequently a theological discipline that is undertaken by *the Church*. This does not preclude those without or within that community of faith from challenging the coherence or the appropriateness of its christological structures. But it remains a reflection on *the Church's* understanding of Jesus, the belief of Christians that the son of Mary is now Lord and Saviour of the world.

Further, christology is concerned with matters of coherence. It must offer a coherent account of how a human life can be identified with the being of God and expounded as the single narrative or history of one person. However, even framing the task in this way can be problematic. It assumes we already have a firm and adequate grasp of what is meant by the being of God, or the defining characteristics of human life or the concept of person, before we even begin our reflection on who Jesus is. But the Church has found that its study of Jesus' reality soon transforms the way it understands the nature of God, or what it means to be truly human, or even what is implied by the notion of person. Nevertheless, the concept of coherence reminds us that christology has to do, at least in part, with holding together a disparate set of realities.

Christology seeks to understand and explain Jesus' person in the context of God's determination to redeem fallen humanity through him. Consequently, it is not possible to detach the discussion of Jesus' being from the grand drama which includes the story of the world's creation by God, its alienation from him and its reconciliation to him through Christ. For, considered on its own, Christ's exalted status is an abstraction. It is made concrete only when understood in relation to the God of Israel and his redemptive action in our history.

To describe christology as the 'faltering' theological exercise of the Church is to recognize, on the one hand, the unfathomable depths of the mystery of its subject matter and, on the other, the difficulty that theologians have always had in providing adequate answers to questions raised about Jesus' person. Most christological formulations in the Church's dogmatic history have been driven by the attempt to solve or eliminate weaknesses apparent in earlier models. Consequently, christology has always had about it the air of a work in progress. As each age brings its own questions, or more often, some-what different slants on ancient questions, so the Church has to be ever ready, if it is to be true to its calling, to address them afresh.

Finally, that the Church struggles in its christological task does not mean the project is not significant. Karl Rahner, the twentieth-century Catholic theologian, is surely right when he described christology, or more precisely the doctrine of the incarnation, in this way:

> It is the very centre of the reality from which we Christians live, of the reality which we believe. For the mystery of the divine Trinity is open to us only here; only here is the mystery of our participation in the divine nature accorded us; and the mystery of the Church is only the extension of the mystery of Christ. Since our faith is contained in this conjunction of mysteries, we should mediate on this centre of theology and of Christian life, and often speak less of a thousand other things. For this mystery is inexhaustible and in comparison with it most of the other things of which we speak are unimportant.[5]

It is difficult to conceive of any significant area of Christian faith or thought that is not dependent on what is held to be true about the person of Christ. Here is the foundation for all the Church's theology and practice, the rationale for its worship and the window for its vision or knowledge of God.

AVOIDING THE ISSUE

There might be some readers who are a little frustrated with the way the task of christology has been introduced in the discussion above. It has been framed as a paradox concerning Jesus' person that is in need of theological explanation. A number of people, however, have a deep and abiding suspicion that the simplicity of Christian faith, outlined in the teaching of Jesus, has from the start suffered serious distortion at the hands of the theologians of the Church. When Jesus' person becomes the subject of metaphysical enquiry and is interpreted in terms of supra-mundane realities or defined with precise technical formulae, their concern is that a particular religious world view or systematizing methodology has somehow been allowed to enter in and distort the simplicity of the Christian message. They would prefer

to speak of Jesus' person in a way that avoids any notion of meta-physical paradox or sometimes even of metaphysics itself. They tend to find themselves, however, in one of two historical positions which do in effect, if not in intention, avoid the inherent metaphysical problem associated with Jesus' person. We can describe them as follows.

Docetism

It is held that the story of Jesus is simply the history of God living among us in human form. The person of Jesus is identified directly with the Lord God Almighty without further qualification. Difficulties with such a view begin to emerge the moment we ask questions of this form: Did Jesus, as God living in our midst, really need to eat and sleep, or wrap a cloak around his body to keep out the cold? Did he suffer any physical or emotional pain? For it appears inconceivable to us that the God who created the heavens and the earth should himself suffer in this way from any physical deprivation? Now if it is argued that: 'He did not really need the blanket or the food or that he did not actually experience physical and emotional pain as we do,' we have a pattern of thought that has historically been described as Docetism. The term is derived from the Greek word '*dokein*' meaning 'to seem' for in such a view Jesus only seems to be human. In reality he is but a manifestation of God living in our midst. His human weaknesses or limitations are more apparent than real. The christological paradox is here avoided by denying or undermining the reality of Jesus' human existence.

Such a way of understanding Jesus is suggested in the reaction that is made to it in later parts of the New Testament:

> Dear friends, do not believe every spirit, but test the spirits to see whether they are from God, because many false prophets have gone out into the world. This is how you can recognize the Spirit of God: Every spirit that acknowledges that Jesus Christ has come in the flesh is from God, but every spirit that does not acknow-ledge Jesus is not from God. (1Jn 4.1–3a)

It was considered by the author of the epistle to be of vital impor-tance for his readers' salvation to affirm that Jesus Christ had com in the flesh, to acknowledge that the manifestation of God amor us was firmly rooted in the reality of corporeal human existenc

A slightly fuller picture of docetic thought can be gathered from the letters of Ignatius bishop of Antioch, written in the early second century as he journeyed to his execution in Rome:

> Stop your ears, therefore, when any one speaks to you at variance with Jesus Christ, who was descended from David, and was also of Mary; who was truly born and did eat and drink. He was truly persecuted under Pontius Pilate; He was truly crucified, and [truly] died. . . . He was also truly raised from the dead. . . . (*Trall.* 9) ANF I, pp. 69, 70

> Now, he suffered all these things for our sakes, that we might be saved. And He suffered truly, even as also He truly raised up Himself, not, as certain unbelievers maintain, that He only seemed to suffer, as they themselves only seem to be [Christians]. (*Smyrn.* 2) ANF I, p. 87

The teaching that Ignatius is countering is that Jesus was not open to the full range of human experiences, in particular that he only seemed to suffer when he was on the cross. Again we find the conviction in Ignatius, as we did among the New Testament authors, that to deny the reality of Jesus' human existence and experience was to jeopardize one's standing as a Christian.

It is unlikely today that any theologians would describe themselves as Docetists or argue that Jesus did not truly suffer in a physical or material body. Rather, the word tends to be used in a pejorative sense to describe christologies which are held to have failed to affirm adequately the human reality of Christ as a fully human physical, mental and spiritual being. D. M. Baillie in his influential book *God was in Christ: An Essay on Incarnation and Atonement* spoke of the Church from the Council of Chalcedon (451) to modern times in this way:

> At any rate it was continually haunted by a docetism which made his human nature very different from ours and indeed largely explained it away as a matter of simulation or 'seeming' rather than reality. Theologians shrank from admitting human growth, human ignorance, human mutability, human struggle and temptation, into their conception of the Incarnate Life, and treated it as simply a divine life lived in a human body (and sometimes even this was conceived as essentially different from our bodies) rather

than a truly human life lived under the psychical conditions of humanity. (p. 11)

And it is in this modified sense that Docetism continues to be an ongoing influence in modern christological discussion.

Ebionitism

The other route taken which avoids the metaphysical problems of christology is to assume that Jesus was no more than a mere man, substantially one with every other human. In historical theology, this view is often associated with an early Christian sect called the Ebionites.

The Ebionites were a community of Jewish-Christians who fled from Jerusalem at the outbreak of the Jewish War (AD66) and moved to Pella in the Transjordan, where they were isolated from the wider church and eventually disappeared from history. They were considered by the mainstream church to be heretical in that they denied both the virgin birth and the divinity of Jesus. Their beliefs are known to us primarily through reference to them in the writings of the Church Fathers. Of their own literature the *Gospel of the Ebionites* is found only in Epiphanius' quotations from it in his *Panarion* written in the fourth century. Epiphanius offers the following summary of their christology:

And on this account they say that Jesus was begotten of the seed of a man, and was chosen; and so by the choice of God he was called the Son of God from the Christ that came into him from above in the likeness of a dove. And they deny that he was begotten of God the Father, but say that he was created as one of the archangels, yet greater, and that he is Lord of the angels and of all things made by the Almighty. (*Panarion* 30.16.4–5) The Apocryphal New Testament translated by Montague Rhode James (Oxford, 1924), p. 10

Now it is notoriously difficult to reconstruct a community's belief system from the literature of its opponents. If, however, Epiphanius is anywhere near the truth in his assessment, the Ebionites held what can be described as an Adoptionist form of christology in that the man Jesus was at some stage in his history adopted into a relation of sonship with God.

The Ebionites have a secure place in historical theology in that they offer an example of a community of Christian believers who from a comparatively early time followed Jesus but, according to the almost unanimous testimony of the Church Fathers who referred to them, did not recognize him to be fully divine. Various groups in more recent times, such as the Socinians, Unitarians and Jehovah's Witnesses, who follow Jesus but openly deny his divinity, look to the Ebionites as a body of disciples whom they hold as being true to the faith as originally given. They see here an early community of Christians who were able to withstand heroically the distorting theological influences of the 'orthodox' church.

Ebionitism has consequently become in christological discussion a convenient term to describe the theory that Jesus is to be conceived of as a mere man. The quotation from Epiphanius, however, suggests that such a label is not entirely fair to them. According to him the Ebionites held that Jesus became the Son of God when the Christ came upon him at baptism. Being lord of all the angels and everything God has made suggests a somewhat higher status for Jesus than that which is normally open to mere men and women. These are in fact quite complex theological and metaphysical ideas and they have far reaching implications for their understanding of the person of Jesus. If this is indeed what the Ebionites believed it is hardly accurate to argue that they conceived of Jesus as no more than a man. Their christology was far from simple and they clearly afforded Jesus an extraordinarily high status.

We have been considering how one might speak of Christ's person without reference to any metaphysical paradox. One route is that of Docetism, a denial of the reality of Jesus' humanity. But it is hard to see how this can be coherently maintained in the light of the testimony of the early Christian disciples to the physicality of his being and the humanity of his thoughts and emotions. The other possibility is to consider Jesus as no more than a man. The problem with this view is that it is simply not compatible with the faith and worship of the Church. Even the Ebionites, the obscure historical group normally cited as the prime exemplars of such a position, do not seem to have subscribed fully to it. Their natural heirs in the seventeenth century, the Socinians, were committed to a thoroughgoing denial of the divinity of Christ and the doctrine of the Trinity. And yet they were formally committed in their church polity to an 'adorationist' position in regard to the worship of Jesus. They believed it was appropriate to adore or worship his person in their hymns and prayers. Within a monotheistic world view, such as that held by the Socinians, such worship is in need of some sort of christological explanation. Paradoxical questions about Jesus' person remain.

CONCLUSION

From its birth the Christian Church has offered divine worship to a young Jewish preacher and miracle-worker who had been executed by the Romans on a charge of insurrection. Trying to make sense of such devotional practice in the context of Jewish monotheism and God's redemptive action provides the impetus for the christological task. We have described it as the faltering attempt of the Church to provide a coherent conceptual and theological explanation of Jesus' person, in harmony with the scriptural testimony, which is able to account for his role in its worship and faith.

Throughout history there have been some who have argued that Jesus was not a real human person and others who have held that he was no more than a man. In both cases the christological problem as such is avoided. But for all those who participate in the life and worship of the Church there does not seem to be any way round this primary question: How can this man who was born of a woman and died under Roman law be worthy of our divine worship, unreserved faith and unquestioned obedience? Reflective Christians are bound to consider seriously the fascinating but perplexing matter of who Jesus really is. Examining how they have in fact done so is the project of this book.

CHAPTER TWO

INCARNATION

EARLY CHRISTIAN REFLECTION ON JESUS

From the time the first worshipping communities came into being, Christians sought ways to speak about Jesus that made sense of his role in both their worship and their experience of salvation. This intention is apparent in all the New Testament authors but most obviously in John, Paul and the writer to the Hebrews. Jesus is identified by them with a variety of Old Testament images and religious concepts to explain why he is indeed God's Messiah, his end-time agent of salvation. Some of these designations such as Daniel's apocalyptic 'Son of Man' came from Jesus' own use of them, but a number of others including John's 'Word of God', Paul's 'second Adam' and Hebrews' 'Melchizedek' were chosen by the Church herself as she reflected on his significance. Each of them contributes to a theological interpretation of Jesus that seeks to explain the saving efficacy of his death and so give adequate grounds for his role as the object of Christian worship. An illuminating example of this is found in a passage from the book of Revelation describing the worship of the heavenly community but which probably also sheds light on the hymnology of the Church at the end of the New Testament period.

> You are worthy to take the scroll
> and to open the seals,
> because you were slain,
> and with your blood you purchased for God
> members of every tribe and language and people and
> nation . . .

Worthy is the Lamb who was slain,
    to receive power and wealth and wisdom and strength
    and honour and glory and praise!

To him who sits on the throne and to the Lamb
    be praise and honour and glory and power,
    for ever and ever. (Rev. 5. 9,12,13)

Jesus is understood as the only one worthy to bring into effect the purposes of God for all future history. By identifying him with the Passover lamb his death is given a theological interpretation. His spilled blood is reckoned to be the ransom payment that will liberate the nations for the service of God. Jesus is consequently deemed to be worthy of every conceivable honour and privilege, and the homage he receives is not differentiated from that which is due to God himself. Jesus stands before the throne of God, distinct from the one who sits upon it and yet sharing equally in all his glory.

There is also a fascinating external, albeit partial, insight into the nature of the early Church's worship in the letter of Pliny the governor of Bithynia to the Roman Emperor Trajan, dated soon after AD 112:

But they [the former Christians] declared that the sum of their guilt or error had amounted only to this, that on an appointed day they had been accustomed to meet before daybreak, and to recite a hymn antiphonally to Christ, as to a god, and to bind themselves by an oath . . . (*Bettenson, Documents of the Early Church* pp. 3–4)

This is not the sort of language that believers are themselves likely to have used in regard to Jesus, but it is how one might have expected outsiders to have interpreted their worship. Hymns were recited to Christ as to a god. Christian reflection on Jesus in those early years had clearly provided a theological rationale for the Church's worship of him as divine.

There was, however, in this initial, formative period another, quite different motivation for reflective consideration of Jesus' person and that was to provide theological grounds for the reality of his human life. This is apparent in the letter to the Hebrews where Jesus' effectiveness as the saviour of humankind is held to be dependent on his full participation in the human condition, physical and spiritual, with all of its frailties:

> Since the children have flesh and blood, he too shared in their humanity so that by his death he might break the power of him who holds he power of death – that is, the devil – and free those who all their lives were held in slavery by their fear of death. For surely it is not angels he helps, but Abraham's descendants. For this reason he had to be made like his brothers and sisters in every way, in order that he might become a merciful and faithful high priest in service to God, and that he might make atonement for the sins of the people. Because he himself suffered when he was tempted, he is able to help those who are being tempted. (Heb. 2.14–18)

This twofold delineation of Jesus by the New Testament Church came to clear expression in a number of the early, post-apostolic writers. Their christological reflection tended to be more analytical and less overtly constructive as the New Testament books came to have an authoritative and determining status equivalent to that of the Jewish Scriptures. In his letter to the Ephesians, written early in the second century, Ignatius (c. 35–c. 107), bishop of Antioch, outlines two distinct sets of apparently opposing attributes that are proper to Jesus:

> There is one Physician who is possessed both of flesh and spirit; both made and not made; God existing in flesh; true life in death; both of Mary and of God; first passible and then impassible, – even Jesus Christ our Lord. (*Eph.* 7) ANF I, p. 52

This somewhat dualistic way of considering Jesus finds its simplest and clearest summary in the words of Irenaeus, the second-century bishop of Lyons. '. . . while He received testimony from all that He was very man, and that He was very God . . . '[6] In this short statement sharp clarity is brought to the christological problem that was to determine the Church's ongoing consideration of the person of Jesus. It generated questions of this form: How are we to conceive of the one person Jesus Christ as being both true man and true God? How can each of these distinct realities be affirmed coherently of a single being? The quotations from Ignatius and Irenaeus are not a solution to the problem, they merely state the case, setting out its parameters. In themselves they lack explanatory power. What the early church was in need of was a way of conceiving how Jesus could be the subject of these two sets of attributes. It did so with the notion of incarnation, derived from the Gospel of John, the narrative of the Word of God becoming flesh, being incarnated among us as a human.

It is well to remind ourselves that this was not the only scripturally based, interpretative scheme open to the Church at the time. There were a range of other perspectives at hand that also brought together the divine and human realities of Jesus' person. These included the biblical testimony that the child born of the virgin Mary was conceived by the Holy Spirit; that in Jesus the fullness of deity lives in bodily form; that as the Spirit came upon Jesus in baptism the Father affirmed him as his divine Son; that Jesus was a man accredited by God by miracles, wonders and signs, which God did through him; that at his resurrection Jesus was declared with power to be the Son of God through the Spirit; and that God was in Christ reconciling the world to himself.

With these and other possibilities before it, why did the Church privilege the one phrase 'the Word became flesh' as the interpretative key to its understanding of the person of Christ and the foundation of its trinitarian thought, a position it held almost unchallenged for the next 1,500 years? Why did it make 'incarnation' its central christological idea and the principal building block of its theology?

IRENAEUS AND THE GNOSTICS

Irenaeus (c. 130–c. 200), the bishop of Lyons, is generally recognized as the first great biblical theologian of the Church. His theological writing was driven by his passion to defend the Church from what he perceived as the deadly errors of Gnosticism. It is difficult for us today to comprehend how the complex, speculative schemes of divine emanations and hidden knowledge put forward by the Gnostics came so close to becoming the Church's dominant theological structure in the second century. Charles Bigg offers an insight into why it was able to exert such power over reflective Christian thought at that time:

It was an attempt, a serious attempt, to fathom the dread mystery of sorrows and pain, to answer that spectral doubt, which is mostly crushed down by force – can the world as we know it have been made by God?[7]

The Gnostic scheme offered a solution to the ever-present problem of God's goodness: How can God be truly good if the world is so obviously evil? Matter itself was generally recognized as liable to corruption and decay, a far remove from the perfect and unchanging immaterial or spiritual nature of God. Gnosticism proposed that the true God was not the one who actually made this world. A distinction was drawn between the God and Father of Jesus and the creator God of the Old Testament, the Demiurge. This distinction was further developed by Marcion (not himself a Gnostic) who argued that the creator God who is revealed in the Jewish Old Testament is a God of law and so antithetically opposed to the God of grace revealed by Jesus.

The key interpretative passage for the christology of a number of the Gnostic thinkers was the anointing of Jesus by the Spirit at his baptism and the ensuing declaration of his divine sonship. Irenaeus offers a summary of their various perspectives:

> For they will have it, that the Word and Christ never came into this world; that the Saviour, too, never became incarnate, nor suffered, but that he descended like a dove upon the dispensational Jesus; and that, as soon as He had declared the unknown Father, he did again ascend into the Pleroma. Some, however, make the assertion, that this dispensational Jesus did become incarnate, and suffered, whom they represent as having passed through Mary just as water through a tube; but others allege him to be the Son of the Demiurge, upon whom the dispensational Jesus descended; while others, again, say that Jesus was born from Joseph and Mary, and that the Christ from above descended upon him, being without flesh, and impassible. But according to the opinion of none of the heretics was the Word of God made flesh. (*Against Heresies* III 10.3) ANF I, p. 427

Irenaeus recognizes that Gnosticism is not able, in any of its various manifestations, to identify the Word of God with frail human flesh with the corruptible material world. Using the anointing of Jesus as their key christological passage allowed the Gnostics to argue that the Word, or Christ, or Saviour merely descends upon the human Jesus at the beginning of his public ministry. The Christ from above and Jesus the man are considered as remaining two quite distinct realities. To concede that the Word of God *was made* flesh, that the good and perfect God became one with the corrupt material world in the person of Jesus Christ, would undermine their whole ontological structure and its clearly distinguished hierarchy of aeons.

Aware of the far-reaching significance of the point at issue Irenaeus argues repeatedly that Jesus Christ is one person

> . . . and that we should not imagine that Jesus was one, and Christ another, but should know them to be one and the same. (Against Heresies III 16.2) ANF I, p. 441 . . . acknowledging that He who is the Son of the Highest, the same is Himself also the son of David. (III 16.3) ANF I, p. 441 . . . foreseeing these blasphemous systems which divide the Lord, as far as lies in their power, saying that He was formed of two different substances. (III 16.5) ANF I, p. 442

And the christological notion which Irenaeus found most conducive to establishing this simple identity was that of incarnation:

> His only-begotten Word, who is always present with the human race, united to and mingled with His own creation, according to the Father's pleasure and who became flesh, is Himself Jesus Christ our Lord, who did also suffer for us, and rose again on our behalf. (III 16.6) ANF I, p. 442

Irenaeus might not have possessed the conceptual tools, developed by the Church as it reflected further on these issues, to explain more clearly the inner logic of the incarnation, but he did affirm its basic reality in uncompromising terms:

> But in every respect, too, he is man, the formation of God; and thus He took up man into Himself, the invisible becoming visible, the incomprehensible being made comprehensible, the impassible become capable of suffering, and the Word being made man, thus summing up all things in Himself. (III 16.6) ANF I, p. 443

The concept of incarnation became in his hands a potent weapon in his battle against the Gnostics. Its widespread acceptance in Christian thought through liturgy, catechism and proclamation played a major part in Gnosticism's final defeat. For the recognition that the Word of God had become flesh and dwelt among us completely undermined the basic presuppositions of Gnostic speculation.

The polemical role played by the idea of incarnation in the writing of Irenaeus not only helps us to understand why it came to assume such a privileged status in the christological thought of the Church, but reminds us of the implications that an incarnational christology has for a Christian doctrine of creation. If the Word of God was truly incarnate, it is not feasible to believe that created matter is in itself evil or that the Father of Jesus is not himself the creator of the cosmos.

INCARNATION AS A MASTER-STORY

There were other currents flowing in the river of Christian thought during the second century that helped to ensure that the concept of incarnation became the dominant christological paradigm for the Church. One of these was the role played by the concept of the '*Logos*', particularly among educated Hellenists, as the inherent principle of reason in the world. The body of Christian writers known as the Apologists, in that they sought to offer a rational defence of the Christian faith, found that this notion served as a helpful bridge in their discussion with their philosophically literate contemporaries. Justin Martyr (*c.*100–*c.*165), one of the foremost of the early Apologists, argued that the presence of the 'germinal' *logos*, the spermatic word, is that which enabled the great poets and philosophers to understand in some measure the things of God. And it was this Word, the inherent principle of reason present among humankind throughout the ages, who had now been incarnated as Jesus Christ for our salvation:

> For each man spoke well in proportion to the share he had of the spermatic word, seeing what was related to it. . . . For next to God, we worship and love the Word who is from the begotten and ineffable God, since also he became man for our sakes, that becoming a partaker of our sufferings, He might also bring us healing. (2. *Apology* 13) ANF I, p. 193

There was clearly much value in using the idea of the Logos to commend Jesus to those who were already familiar with the term from the writings of the Stoics, Philo or late Judaism. It also meant that the narrative of the Logos' incarnation as outlined in the prologue of John's Gospel became a helpful way to explain Jesus' person.

We could say the narrative of the incarnation of the Word of God came to function in the christological thought of the early church as a 'master-story'. All other accounts of Jesus' relation to God came to be subsumed and interpreted under this determinative explanatory narrative. It was the Church's commitment to this particular story that shaped the trinitarian theology of the Church and provided the conceptual framework for the christological settlements of Nicea and Chalcedon. But this was also a story that generated its own baffling questions and paradoxes – questions which were to engage the mind of thoughtful Christians in serious debate for the next 300 years and more. Two of the most immediate of these had to do with the pre-existence of the one who became Jesus and the idea of some sort of transformation in the being of God.

THE PRE-EXISTENT WORD

To hold that the divine Word became flesh is to imply that the Word has a prior existence external to the incarnation. But if the 'Word' is a pre-existing reality what are we to say of its relation to God? Is the 'Word' simply another name for God or are these two to be differentiated in some way? And how can they be so distinguished without undermining the primary axiom of monotheism – that God is one?

Attentive to these concerns, the Apologists sought to describe the relation of the Word to God in a manner that safeguarded both the indivisible nature of God's being and the distinct reality of the Word. They argued that the 'Word' was God's own word or reason, inhering in God's person but coming to external expression in creation and incarnation. The analogy with human reason and speech helped them to conceive how the Word might be inseparable from God's being and yet, once spoken, become a reality in some way distinct from him:

> . . . for when we give out some word, we beget the word; yet not by abscission, so as to lessen the word [which remains] in us, when we give it out: and just as we see also happening in the case of a fire, which is not lessened when it has kindled [another], but remains the same; and that which has been kindled by it likewise

appears to exist by itself, not diminishing that from which it was kindled. (*Dial.* 61) ANF I, p. 227

There is no diminution in the being of God having spoken the Word or having sent him forth as the agent of creation. And so we find here in the second century a fairly sophisticated attempt to provide an intellectually satisfying account of the nature of the Word, that is, the one who was to become Jesus.

Of course much more still needs to be said about the ontology of the Word and the relation it has to its divine source. For instance, Justin Martyr's account above suggests that the Word only became a reality in some way distinct from God in the acts of creation and incarnation – when the Word was spoken. Paul of Samosata, the bishop of Antioch, went further and seemed to do away completely with any distinction between the Word and God. He argued that the Word was not a self-subsistent being but referred simply to God's commandment or ordinance. At the Council of Antioch in 268 Paul of Samosata's position was condemned by the bishops present. The Church was determined to make clear that the Word who took human flesh was not merely God's verbal utterance lacking any subsistence of its own, but a pre-existent, self-subsistent reality that nevertheless did not undermine monotheism. This is what a doctrine of incarnation was seen as implying, and it was within this framework that the ongoing discussion was conducted. The other perplexing problem that arose from the notion of incarnation was that of divine transformation.

DOES GOD CHANGE?

Irenaeus had written boldly about the invisible becoming visible and the impassible becoming capable of suffering in the event of the incarnation. The question that arises naturally from such an account is 'Does the Word of God change in the process of becoming human?' Does becoming man imply some alteration in the divine being? Christian theology over the ages has struggled to give a definitive answer to this deceptively simple question.

The traditional response of the Church has been to assert that God as God does not change. The difficulty is that an incarnational christology appears to require alteration in God of a quite radical sort: the Word *became* flesh. Does not this *becoming* imply a transformation of the divine person? How apart from change can the invisible become visible, the incomprehensible be made comprehensible, the impassible become capable of suffering? Nevertheless, philosophically aware Christians have generally been reluctant to concede that God is, properly speaking, open to substantial change in this way.

To defend its view of the immutability of God's being, the early Church was eventually compelled to modify Irenaeus' strong language about the notion of becoming. Athanasius, who we shall discuss more fully in the next chapter, put forward a more nuanced explanation of the incarnation, as he sought to safeguard the true divinity of the pre-existent Christ:

> [In] the same way it is possible in the Lord's instance also to understand aright, that He did not become other than Himself on taking the flesh, but, being the same as before, he was robed in it; and the expressions 'He became' and 'He was made,' must not be understood as if the Word, considered as the Word, were made, but that the Word, being Framer of all, afterwards was made High Priest, by putting on a body which was originate and made, and such as he can offer for us; wherefore He is said to be made. (*Contra Arius* 2.8) NPNF 2nd IV, p. 352

Athanasius recognized that to say that the Word of God 'put on a human body', or 'was robed in flesh', is less open to misinterpretation than the statement that 'he became or was made flesh.' As the theological dangers from unguarded language became increasingly apparent in the christological discussions of the time, the Church found itself compelled to use more precise theological terminology to protect the truth about the person of Jesus. In due course even the idea of 'being clothed with a human body' was recognized as an inadequate way of expressing the reality of the humanity of Jesus and the normative way of describing the incarnation was of 'the Word of God assuming or taking human nature to himself'. This concern to safeguard the ontological immutability of the Word in the act of incarnation led in due course to a detailed consideration of what was meant by the human and divine natures of Christ and how their relation was to be understood. Every forward step in the christological discussion appeared to generate a new set of questions for further consideration.

We catch a glimpse, even in this cursory sketch, of the Church's determination to speak with considered precision about the person of Christ. Why had this become a matter of such weight among reflective Christians? Why was it so important for the Church to be correct in what it believed and taught about Jesus' nature or being? In short, why had the issues of christology become the focus of so much theological attention in the life of the Christian community?

The early Church had come to recognize that its understanding of the person of Jesus was the cornerstone of its entire belief system, its worship and its way of life. Everything of importance that it held to be true was seen to depend on who Jesus Christ was. Consequently, understanding and confessing Jesus aright was for these Christians far more than a mark of ecclesiastical orthodoxy; it was for them the basis or ground of their salvation. They believed that to be wrong here threatened their eternal standing with God. Historical theologians who interpret the christological debates of the early centuries simply as a matter of power politics, Machiavellian intrigue and party spirit are in danger of completely missing the point. For most Christians these discussions were related to eternal salvation. Heretical teaching was generally considered as deadly poison to the soul:

> Flee for your very life from these men; they are poisonous growths with a deadly fruit, and one taste of it is speedily fatal. (Ignatius, *Trall.*11) Early Christian Writings: The Apostolic Fathers, translated by Maxwell Staniforth (London, Penguin Books, 1980) p. 98

Consequently, the truth about Jesus' person was held to be of ultimate soteriological significance. That is why it was so important to get it right.

CONCLUSION

From the start Christians found themselves reflecting theologically on the person of Jesus so that they might explain how he was the agent of God's end-time act of salvation and the appointed plenipotentiary of his divine Kingdom. In this process they came to recognize the need to affirm of him the dual reality, that he was both true man and true God. To conceive how these disparate realities could be affirmed of one person, the Church privileged the Johannine notion of incarnation as its principal interpretive tool: the Word became flesh and lived among us, or more precisely, the Word of God assumed human nature to himself and without change to his own being became fully man. Particular care was taken in such formulations because the Church believed that a correct (orthodox) understanding of the person of Jesus was the foundation for a proper appreciation of the Gospel and so of eternal salvation. It was this deep concern about salvation that fuelled the Arian debate, the most significant controversy over the person of Christ in the life of the Church.

CHAPTER THREE

ATHANASIUS AND THE ARIANS

The concept of incarnation, adopted by the Church as its primary interpretive model, has provided the framework within which the person of Jesus Christ has been explained for the greater part of its history. Within this structure it was the Arian controversy that led to the formulation of the principal symbol of Christian orthodoxy, the Nicene Creed, and supplied the building blocks for the distinctive Christian interpretation of the nature of God. The debate Athanasius had with the Arians has therefore a fair claim to being the most influential theological discussion in the Church's reflective life.

For some 60 years the Arian controversy disturbed the ecclesiastical harmony, such as it was, of the ancient Christian world. From about 320 when Alexander, Arius' bishop, condemned his teaching at a synod in Alexandria, until the first Council of Constantinople in 381 which heralded the final victory of the 'orthodox' position, the fortunes of both parties fluctuated from council to council according to the theological inclination of the various emperors, the relative political strength of the opposing parties and the persuasive power of the respective arguments. The use of the word 'orthodox' in this context is of course anachronistic. For commentators at the time, it must have been far from clear which of the parties would finally triumph and so prove to be heir to the title. In hindsight historians today often speak of the teaching that opposed the Arians as 'Alexandrian episcopal orthodoxy', highlighting not only its ultimate success but also the fact that its two leading exponents were the Alexandrian Bishops Alexander and Athanasius.

What was the argument all about? Before seeking to answer this it is helpful to remind ourselves what the opposing parties had in common. Both offered divine honour to Jesus Christ in their worship;

both interpreted his person within an incarnational framework whereby a pre-existent being became a human person; both recognized the Scriptures as having final authority in their interpretation of Jesus and both also sought to strengthen their arguments with support from the writings of the Fathers. On what then did they disagree? Greg and Groh in their sympathetic study *Early Arianism: A View of Salvation* opened their illuminating work with this incisive analysis:

> Everyone familiar with the early Arian writings knows the large claims made by them for the redeemer. He is (the only begotten god) or just (the only begotten); he is a 'strong god', a god from above, unchangeable and unalterable, the 'power' of God, the word of God, wisdom of God, and so forth. But if all the criticism levelled at the Arian representation of Christ by Bishops Alexander and Athanasius, both of Alexandria, could be reduced to a single line, it would read like this: no matter how the Arians huff and puff, what they preach is a creature promoted to the status of a god. The Alexandrian bishops had it exactly right. The Arian Christ was a 'creature' or a 'work' of God the Creator who had been promoted to the rank of a divine son and redeemer. (p. 1)

Why should this theory have had such extraordinary persuasive power in the Church at that time? Why 1,200 years later, in the somewhat modified form of Continental Socinianism, did it prove to be so serious a challenge to the orthodox doctrine of the Trinity? Why was Arianism to receive such strong support in eighteenth-century England from the physicist Isaac Newton and a number of influential Anglican clergy? Why do strains of it continually reappear in reconstructed forms of Adoptionism in the theology of prominent British theologians? And the answer, which might be somewhat disquieting for those holding an 'orthodox' view, is that there is much in the New Testament portrayal of the nature of redemption, the person of Jesus Christ and the work of the Holy Spirit that would appear to give support to the position of the Arians.

AN ARIAN ACCOUNT OF SALVATION

The creaturely status of the pre-existent Christ, although serving as the defining characteristic of Arian thought, can be viewed as an outcome rather than the driving force of its theology. It is a conclusion required by other more primary concerns. One of these is the Arian view of salvation.

The Arians understood divine salvation as a solution to the problem of moral wilfulness rather than of human mortality and creaturely corruption. They held that the predicament in which we all find ourselves derives from our disobedience to the will of God. Jesus came to share in our creatureliness and in such a condition learnt and practised obedience to the Father. His life of increasing faithfulness is the ground of his own elevation to divine sonship by adoption.

> ... as foreknowing that He would be good, did God by anticipation bestow on Him this glory, which afterwards, as man, He attained from virtue. (Athanasius quoting Arius in *Contra Arius* 1:5) NPNF 2nd IV, p. 309

> The Unbegun made the Son a beginning of things originated; and advanced Him as a Son to Himself by adoption. (Athanasius quoting Arius in *De Synodis* 15:3) NPNF 2nd IV, p. 457

This idea of the Saviour's development or growth in status and reward of divine sonship from the Father was believed by the Arians to be reflected in a number of New Testament texts including Heb. 1.4. 'So he *became* as much superior to the angels as the name he has inherited is superior to theirs.' Through his obedience to God's will, Jesus was viewed as the paradigm or model of salvific possibilities open to us as we share in his life of faithfulness and so participate in his adoptive sonship. The predominant characteristic of Jesus as the divine servant is his free submission to his Father's will in a life open to suffering, temptation and change.

In sharp contrast, Alexandrian episcopal orthodoxy emphasized what is sometimes described as a 'physical' theory of the atonement. Through the incarnation, Christ brings incorruptibility and immortality to our creaturely bodies:

> ... that it was in the power of none other to turn the corruptible to incorruption, except the Saviour Himself, that had at the beginning also made all things out of nought; and that none other could create anew the likeness of God's image for men, save the Image of the Father; and that none other could render the mortal immortal, save our Lord Jesus Christ, Who is the Very Life ... (Athanasius, *On the Incarnation* 20) NPNF 2nd IV, p. 47

There are other aspects to Athanasius' soteriology including those of Christ as a sacrifice for our sins and as a ransom for our lives. But in his theology it is the physical theory which plays the dominant role in determining the metaphysical status of Jesus' pre-existent personage to be one of true divinity.

Greg and Groh helpfully summarize the distinctive feature of the Arian theory of salvation: 'Perfection is understood in terms of the community of will and covenantal obedience, not in terms of the renovation and metastasis of creaturely essence' (p. 67). It means that salvation is accomplished through the obedient life of Jesus and the moral transformation that flows from it rather than through the act of incarnation and the renovation our being.

Now the reader will be aware that this Arian understanding of the human predicament and of divine salvation in terms of ethical rather than ontological categories has much in the Scriptures to commend it. The Arian scheme fails to give due emphasis to the concepts of grace, mercy and forgiveness for the ungodly but it does find considerable support in the biblical witness for its affirmation that our human plight derives from our unwillingness to obey God rather than from the limitations of our creaturely constitution and subjection to mortality.

JESUS AND THE HOLY SPIRIT

From Athanasius we learn that the Arians believed Jesus to be dependent on the Holy Spirit for his own spirituality, growth in grace and consequent inhabitation of the Father:

> . . . except they shall dare, as commonly, so now to say, that the Son also by participation of the Spirit and by improvement of conduct came to be himself also in the Father. But here again is an excess of irreligion, even in admitting the thought. For He, as has been said, gives to the Spirit, and whatever the Spirit hath, He hath from the Word. (Athanasius *Contra Arius* 3:24) NPNF 2nd IV, p. 407

In contrast to the Arian position Athanasius believes that Christ's divine being does not allow Jesus in his life among us to require or need the Holy Spirit either in his relation with his Father or in his public ministry. It is rather the divine Word who gives from himself to the Spirit and also dispenses the Spirit to us. His commitment to such a position means that Athanasius has to resort to a rather forced exegesis in order to explain what actually happened when the Spirit descended upon Jesus at his baptism:

> If then for our sake He sanctifies Himself, and does this when He is become man, it is very plain that the Spirit's descent on Him in Jordan was a descent upon us, because of His bearing our body. And it did not take place for promotion to the Word, but again for our sanctification that we might share his anointing, and of us it might be said, 'Know ye not that ye are God's Temple, and the Spirit of God dwelleth in you?' For when the Lord, as man, was washed in Jordan, it was we who were washed in Him and by Him. And when He received the Spirit, we it was who by Him were made recipients of it. (Athanasius *Contra Arius* 1:47) NPNF 2nd IV, p. 333

Athanasius is not able to concede that Jesus in his own person and for his own good was in any way comforted, guided, empowered, enabled, sanctified or encouraged by the Holy Spirit. It is a position that certainly appears to run against the plain reading of the Gospel narratives.

Among the Arians, Jesus' anointing by the Holy Spirit was but one aspect of their broader view that the high status and authority of Jesus came to be his by gift from the Father rather than by nature. Athanasius details their arguments:

> How can the Son be from the Father by nature, and be like him in essence, who says 'All power is given unto Me;' and 'The Father judgeth no man, but hath committed all judgment unto the Son;' and 'The Father loveth the Son, and hath given all things into His hand.' (*Contra Arius* 3:26) NPNF 2nd IV, p. 407

Their point is that in the Scriptures the Son's high status is dependent on the Father's pleasure rather than being a natural consequence of the Son's essential divinity. If it is something he has been given then he clearly does not have it by nature, that is, from his being or essence. In short, if the Word were true God why should he need to be *given* these things by the Father?

Athanasius offers alternative ways of interpreting the array of Scriptures which the Arians had put forward to show that Jesus' status was dependent on the Father's good will. Two are of particular significance. First he refers such experiences of Jesus to his humanity. That the Word truly became flesh or man means that much of what happened to Jesus is appropriately described as having taken place 'in the flesh'. For instance in the first epistle of Peter it is said that 'he suffered in the flesh' (1 Pet. 4.1). So it might be argued that he received an exalted status from the Father 'in the flesh', that is, in his humanity:

> For on this account has the Apostle himself said 'Christ then having suffered', not in his Godhead but 'for us in the flesh,' that these affections may be acknowledged as, not proper to the very Word by nature, but proper by nature to the very flesh. (*Contra Arius* 3:34) NPNF 2nd IV, p. 412

Athanasius' second mode of responding to these texts is more problematic. He concedes that everything that the Word has comes from the Father, but argues that it has been received by him from the Father eternally. At the heart of his christology lies the idea that the Son's essence and therefore his divine status is eternally derived from the Father. The difficulty with such a notion when applied to texts of this sort: 'The Father loves the Son, and has given all things into his hand,' is that it suggests that the status of the Son comes from a voluntary decision of the Father, albeit eternally, rather than from the Son's essential being. And such a concession, as we shall see, plays into the hands of the Arians.

THE WILL OF GOD

The Arians held that the primary attribute of God in determining his relation with creation is his will. Men and women, including Christ, are brought into close relation with God by conformity to the divine will through the exercise of their own free volition (see Greg and Groh p. 8). And this freedom to sin or not to sin, to obey or not to obey indicates a radical openness to change both in Christ and in all other creatures. Within this conceptual framework, God's Word is held by the Arians to be the pronouncement of God's will, a verbalization of the divine volition, something as distinct from the essence

of God as the syllables of a man's utterance are from his being. It is
a perspective that Athanasius strongly opposes:

> And man's word is composed of syllables, and neither lives nor
> operates anything, but is only significant of the speaker's intention,
> and does but go forth and go by, no more to appear, since it was not
> at all before it was spoken; wherefore the word of man neither lives
> nor operates anything, nor in short is man. And this happens to it,
> as I said before, because man who begets it, has his nature out of
> nothing. But God's Word is not merely pronounced, as one may
> say, nor a sound of accents, nor by His Son is meant His command;
> but as radiance of light, so is He perfect offspring from perfect.
> Hence He is God also, as being God's Image; for the Word was
> God, says Scripture. (*Contra Arius* 2:35) NPNF 2nd IV, p. 367

The Arians operated 'with a scheme of divine command and creaturely response which conceived of the Word of God in voluntaristic
rather than hypostasised categories' (Greg and Groh p. 26). We might
say that Jesus was understood to be one with the Father in the sense
of harmony or agreement, or perhaps even conformity of action,
rather than having the same being or identity.

In Arian thought, the primary place of the will in the divine attributes meant that the Son was considered to be the outcome of the
Father's volition. 'Arius, Eusebius, and Asterius with one voice describe
the Son's creation as an act of the Father's will and portray the Son as
a product of the Father's intentionality. Their insistence that "the Son
has received being from the Father at his will and pleasure (*boulesai
kai thelesei*)" insures God's own freedom to act – it is the counterpart
to the Christology of promotion. "Unless", the Arians maintain, "he
[the Son] has by will come to be, then God has a Son by necessity and
against his good pleasure"' (Greg and Groh p. 92). Athanasius seeks
to counter their position by arguing that what flows from nature or
essence is not contrary to will but prior to it, thus transcending it
(see Athanasius *Contra Arius* 3:62), NPNF 2nd IV, p. 427–428

For the Arians the Son is fashioned by God as an instrument to
bring into effect the divine will through the creation of the cosmos
and of humankind.

> 'Then wishing to form us, thereupon He made a certain one, and
> named him Word and Wisdom and Son, that he might form us by
> means of Him.' (*Contra Arius* 1:5) NPNF 2nd IV, p. 309

But it is at this point that the Arian logic breaks down, as Athanasius was quick to show (see *Contra Arius* 3:61,62). According to the Arians all of creation comes into being through the will or good pleasure of God, that is, through his Will or Word. The 'Word' is here understood by the Arians as the verbalization of the divine volition and not as a substantial entity. But then alongside the divine Will, the pre-existent Christ, a created being, is also held to be the chosen agent of creation and so also the Word of God. This created being is spoken of as the 'Word' in that he partakes in the divine volition. We have here what is sometimes referred to as an unnecessary multiplication of entities. There is neither necessity nor space for two quite distinct Words of God serving as creative agents in John's Logos theology. One of them is, so to speak, redundant. A major weakness in Arianism is bound up with its postulation of a creaturely pre-existent Word substantially distinct from God's creative Will or Word.

THE PRE-EXISTENT CHRIST

Arian christology affirmed a doctrine of the incarnation and with it the reality of the pre-existent Son. Opponents of Arianism have often suggested that in doing so they posited a being who was neither truly God nor truly creature, a *tertium quid*, a third sort of metaphysical entity lying somewhere between creator and creation. This does not appear to be the case. The evidence before us is that the Arians argued consistently that the pre-existent Son was a creature, formed by the will of God, who did not in any respect share in the divine essence. He is a son by adoption as we are; he is divinized by participation in the divine being through the Holy Spirit precisely as we might be. All his high titles are the rewards he received from the Father with a view to the purity of the life he was to lead. They are, as it were, honorary titles rather than descriptions of his being. In Arianism there is, in fact, no blurring of the distinction between the true God and his creation, even though the repeated ascription of the title 'god' to Jesus and other created beings might sometimes seem to suggest it. Whatever divine status might be attributed to Christ by the Arians, it is one that always lies firmly within the possibilities appropriate for a creature. He is not the 'true' God. It is this consistency in their ontology that highlights the fatal flaw in the Arian system. That a created being should be the direct agent of both the creation of the world and the salvation of humankind is simply not credible within the monarchical interpretation of God which the Christian church shares with Judaism.

Further, although the Arians can find scriptural warrant for calling creatures 'sons of God' they struggle to show why the Scriptures should consider Christ to be the 'unique' son or the 'only-begotten' son. They did believe that he was created directly by God while we have all been created through the Son. But having argued that Christ is like us in every way, they have no strategy or even inclination to explain why he is, in some respect, absolutely different from us. In short, they are not able to account for his particular being, a concept that is central to the New Testament presentation of Jesus' person: 'Moses was faithful as a *servant* in all God's house, testifying to what would be said in the future. But Christ is faithful as a *son* over God's house' (Heb. 3.5,6a). Even Moses does not share in Jesus' unique filial relation to God.

Finally, if all the divine titles that are ascribed to Jesus refer to the honorary status that he, a creature, has received from God, it is difficult to understand why it is appropriate for the Church to worship him. One is able to sympathize with Athanasius and others, opponents of Arianism who held it to be the height of blasphemy to offer a creature, however exalted, the reverence and praise that is due to God alone? If the Church was right to honour Christ, as it had been doing in its liturgy and worship, then he was surely more than a mere creature.

AN ONTOLOGICAL RELATIONSHIP

The Arians spoke of the divinity of Christ in terms of his conformity to the divine will, his participation in the life of God and his pre-eminent status, received by way of the Father's good pleasure. But all these fell short of indicating that his own nature or being was anything other than that of a creature. The orthodox party recognized that to defend the true divinity of Christ they would need to argue that he shared in God's essence or being.

How was one to conceive of the pre-existent Christ as distinct from God and yet sharing his essence? A favoured analogy of the orthodox was that of creaturely generation. As humans derive their being from their parents so Christ was held to derive his being from that of God. The widespread use of Father and Son language in the

New Testament gave material support to their argument. Human parenting, however, remains but an analogy. The pre-existent Christ is not 'born' of God in a way that might suggest two parents. He is rather held to have been eternally 'generated' by the Father alone and any idea of sexuality in God is clearly avoided. In a number of respects his coming into being is not related to human parenting at all. Nevertheless, the metaphor of parent does provide a way of conceiving how the Father might be both logically prior to the Son and the source of his being without any diminution of his own essence. It also implies that the being of the Son is of the same order as that of the Father. Other popular metaphors among the 'orthodox' for the relationship of the pre-existent Christ to God were those of a light ray to its light source and a stream to a fountain. Such ideas suggest the distinction between Father and Son, the logical priority of the Father, the Son's dependence on the Father for his being and the close similarity of their respective natures.

The problem with the idea of sonship in the debate was that the Arians happily affirmed that Christ was the Son of the Father without conceding that he was of the Father's essence. They argued, as we have seen, that Christ was a son by adoption. The 'orthodox' were in dire need of a concept that related the Son to the Father and unambiguously excluded an Arian interpretation. They found it in the word 'homoousion' which can be interpreted as 'of the same essence or substance'. The term suffered from the novelty of its use in a theological context and its lack of scriptural support. Nevertheless, its value in safeguarding the true divinity of the Son appeared to the 'orthodox' to outweigh the disadvantages accruing from the charge of theological innovation. Originally, they used it to indicate that the Father and Son shared the same sort of being. Later it was recognized that 'sameness of essence' logically implied that they were of one single substance.

The appeal of the term 'homoousion' lay in its simplicity and its power to exclude an Arian interpretation. No true Arian was able to affirm that the Son was of one substance with the Father. The term could not be glossed or qualified in a way which allowed an interpretation of the Son as no more than a mere creature. And so the 'homoousion' came to have determinative power not only in the Church's christology but also in her understanding of God. In the phraseology of the Nicene Creed, or more precisely of the

Nicene–Constantinopolitan Creed, we catch a glimpse of the role of the 'homoousion', along with other key concepts, in the formulation of the orthodox position:

We believe in one Lord, Jesus Christ
the only Son of God.
eternally begotten of the Father,
God from God, Light from Light,
true God from true God,
begotten not made,
of one being (*homoousion*) with the Father;
through him all things were made.

CONCLUSION

The Arian debate focused the Church's attention on the need to define clearly the nature of Jesus' divinity. The difficulty was that there seemed to be nothing in the language of the Scriptures to denote his status which could not also be interpreted in an Arian sense to imply that he was no more than the most exalted of creatures. And yet the biblical witness to his role as creator and redeemer of the world; his unique relation to the Father and his high status as the proper object of Christian worship required, in a monotheistic context, that he be considered as one with the Father in his divinity. The term *homoousion* was consequently employed by the 'orthodox' to safeguard this divine identity. And from that time this concept became a vital building block in Christian theological construction, in particular its conceptual formulation of a trinitarian understanding of God.

However, it was soon realized that such an unambiguous affirmation of Christ's deity would require much more careful thought as to what could be properly said of his human life among us and the nature of the relation between the two. And it is this subject which dominated Christian theological reflection for the next 400 years.

CHAPTER FOUR

THE HUMAN MIND OF THE WORD OF GOD

In the first centuries of its life the Church spent a great deal of its time and energy attempting to bring a measure of coherence to its conception of the person of Jesus. This reflective process progressed through a number of fairly well-defined phases. Once an issue had been settled to its general satisfaction, the focus of the Church's attention tended to shift to the new set of questions arising out of the previous consensus.

Here is a summary sketch of the initial stages of this process. The early Christians inherited a monotheistic understanding of God. Only the creator God, the God of Abraham, Isaac and Jacob was held to be worthy of any form of divine worship. However, after Jesus' resurrection the first disciples began to offer this Galilean Jew an extraordinary measure of divine honour. There are no indications that this devotional practice was considered among themselves to be at all problematic or at odds with their monotheistic commitment. The momentous events of Easter and these early Christians' own personal experience of salvation appeared to demand it of them. When serious debate over Christ's person became an issue towards the end of the first century it had to do not with his divine status and the resulting challenge to monotheism but with the materiality of his body. Committed to the reality of Jesus' physical being, the Church made it a credal requirement to confess that the Word of God had truly come in the flesh. Being worthy of divine honour did not mean for Christians that Jesus Christ was not also a real human.

This double perspective, although present from the beginning, came to clear articulation in the mid-second century in the assertion of Irenaeus that Jesus was both 'true God and true man'. The primary scriptural model adopted by the Church to conceptualize this dual consideration of Christ's person was that of incarnation. Jesus was considered as the 'enfleshment' of the divine Word. Such a claim was recognized as implying that a 'pre-existent being' had come to live among us as a man. Consequently, those christologies which denied his pre-existence (Adoptionist) were in due course formally rejected. The critical question which then faced the Church concerned the nature of this pre-existent being. Was he the most exalted of creatures or was he truly God? After protracted debate with the Arians a settlement was finally achieved in a credal formula of immense significance that he, the Son, was of one substance (*homoousion*) with God the Father, having been eternally generated from his being.

Such a resolution did not, however, bring an end to the discussion. Nicea generated its own set of fresh questions. If Christ was of one substance with God the Father, what was to be said about the nature of his life and actions as an itinerant healer and teacher in the Roman province of Palestine? Did he need to pray? How could it be that he claimed not to know everything? As we might put it today: were Jesus' thoughts those of a first-century Jewish man informed and conditioned by the social and religious world view of his community or were they those of an omniscient divine being? Did he have a reflective mental-life anything like our own?

APOLLINARIUS (c. 310–c. 390)

One branch of contemporary Greek philosophy envisioned the Logos or Word as the personal governing principle which provides and gives life to the whole of creation. It was a concept which a number of Christian thinkers were happy to work with and develop. Athanasius envisioned the Logos' action with respect to Jesus' human nature as just one aspect of his wider work, similar in some respects to that of the soul to the body. In fact, Athanasius often refers to the physical body of Jesus as the instrument of the Word which he graphically portrays as being wielded by him. In all this the agent of Jesus' human nature is clearly the Word, while his humanity is the instrument through which he acts. J. N. D. Kelly aptly describes this relation: 'the Word for Athanasius was the governing principle, or *hegemonikon*, in Jesus Christ, the subject of all the sayings, experiences and actions attributed to the Gospel figure.'[8]

However, with such an uncompromising conception of the eternal Son's determination of Jesus' life, some explanation was needed to account for the human frailties and sufferings which the Gospels attribute to him. Athanasius did so by ascribing all these to his flesh:

> [I]n nature the Word Himself is impassible, and yet because of that flesh which he put on, these things are ascribed to Him, since they are proper to the flesh, and the body itself is proper to the Saviour.[9]

Some things then are spoken of him as God and others of him as 'He that bore flesh.' Athanasius suggests it is a fairly straightforward matter to distinguish between these two. 'For if we recognize what is proper to each, and see and understand that both these things and those are done by One, we are right in our faith, and shall never stray.'[10]

This explanation does not fit as awkwardly with his original position as it might first appear, particularly if we remember that Athanasius viewed the relation of the Word to humanity as similar to the Platonic understanding of the relation of soul and body. We simply have to recognize what belongs to each. Today we might say that a person's mental and physical faculties are distinguishable and yet remain the faculties of the one person. A difficulty, however, arises when we consider Christ's frailties, not merely in his physical body or in his emotions, but in his intellect, will and spirituality. Is it possible that Christ's knowledge was limited? Athanasius' model does not allow him to ascribe such limitations to the flesh, for these are functions not of the instrument but of him who wields it. But neither would it be proper to refer such frailty to the perfect nature of the divine Son. This is a point of weakness in Athanasius' christology. In order to be consistent he is forced to be less than fair with the passages in Scripture which speak of Jesus growing in wisdom and grace or lacking complete knowledge.[11]

Apollinarius of Laodicea was a close friend of Athanasius and shared in his theological perspective. He was deeply committed to safeguarding the doctrine of the Son's substantial unity with the Father, embodied in the Nicene Creed. He was also opposed to the dualistic direction taken by the Antiochene school with its emphasis on two distinct natures in the incarnate Christ. Against this two-nature view he emphasized the unity of Christ's being. However, what was implied in Athanasius' christology was now made explicit by Apollinarius. He argued that the Word, as the governing principle of the life of the incarnate Christ, took the place of the human mind or soul in Jesus. The Logos was both the intelligent principle directing his life and also the animating spirit of his flesh.

Apollinarius' theory was not a heavy-handed attempt to remove all subtlety or nuance from the problem of christology. It was, rather, the work of a careful theologian who had probably gone further than any before him in his consideration of agency in the life of Christ. His conclusion is a logical outcome of the direction taken by what has become known as the Alexandrian school with its emphasis on the integrity of Christ's being, its commitment to the substantial unity of the Son with the Father and its use of a Word–flesh model for Christ's person. Commentators have recognized that this school tended to understand the incarnation as the assumption by the divine Logos of 'human flesh', rather than the unity of the Logos with a 'man'. Apollinarius strongly opposed the Word–man christological theory favoured by the competing school of thought, known as the Antiochenes. He believed that the idea that the Word united himself with a man was incorrigibly dualistic and that it was wrong to speak of Christ's body and the divine Word as distinct natures. Rather, he held that in the incarnation the flesh and the godhead were fused into one single nature, one life, one *hypostasis* in Jesus Christ.

Apollinarius believed that such a christological perspective required the divine Word to have actually replaced the human soul or mind in Christ. The Logos, or governing principle of the universe was envisioned by him as the only animating spirit of the incarnate Christ's being. It is, of course, a highly problematic proposal and was quite quickly recognized to be so by the Church. If Christ did not have a human mind or soul it was difficult to conceive how he could be a human at all. It meant that in the incarnation the Word had assumed an incomplete human nature to himself. But if this is the case the question was asked: how can we be saved? It was recognized that it is our minds and not merely our bodies that are in need of redemption:

If anyone had put his trust in him as a man without a human mind, he is really bereft of mind and quite unworthy of salvation.

For that which he has not assumed, he has not healed; but that which is united to his Godhead, is also saved. If only half Adam fell, then that which Christ assumes and saves may be half also; but if the whole of Adam fell, he must be united to the whole nature of him that was begotten, and so be saved as a whole. (Gregory of Nazianzen, *Epistle to Cledonius* 184) NPNF 2nd VII, p. 440

At the Council of Alexandria in 362 a christological perspective closely related to that of Apollinarius was opposed. Alerted to Apollinarius' doctrine, Pope Damasus called a synod in Rome in 377 which resulted in an outright condemnation of his teaching. This decision was upheld by synods in Alexandria and Antioch and finally by the Council of Constantinople in 381. In 388 an imperial decree was issued:

We command that the Apollinarians and all other followers of diverse heresies shall be prohibited from all places, from the walls of the cities, from the congregations of honourable men, from the communion of saints. They shall not have the right to ordain clerics, they shall forfeit the privilege of assembling congregations either in public or private churches. (*Codex Theodosius* XVI) Creeds, Councils and Controversies: Documents illustrative of the history of the Church A.D. 337–461, ed. by J. Stevenson (London, SPCK, 1966) p. 101

Apollinarius, a great defender of orthodoxy in the Arian debate and close friend of Athanasius, had put forward a coherent and brilliantly constructed theory concerning agency in the life of Jesus Christ. He proposed that the Word was not only the single animating principle of his being but also the lone agent of all his thoughts, knowledge and decisions. In effect, there was no human mind or soul in Christ. To the question which we raised at the beginning of this section: 'Did Jesus have a reflective mental-life anything like ours?' his answer was an unambiguous No!

It was, however, a position that the major theological schools and courts of the Church were united in rejecting. And this condemnation of his position has been upheld by the major branches of the Church throughout its ongoing history. Apollinarianism is clearly not an option open to the Church. Jesus Christ did have a human mind, because he was fully human. However, as we shall see, the implications arising from this apparently simple proposition are not that easy to incorporate within the framework of the Nicene settlement.

ALEXANDRIANS AND ANTIOCHENES

The Alexandrians faithfully followed the Nicene Creed in their interpretation of Jesus Christ as the incarnation of the divine Word of God. He is the only begotten Son of God, of one substance with the Father, who for our salvation has humbled himself and become one of us by taking our complete nature to himself. He is the agent of our salvation. The Word does not have a relation with a man called Jesus as, for instance, the Holy Spirit might indwell one of the prophets. He is that person. This is the essence of Alexandrian christology and it was seen as flowing logically from the theology which prevailed at Nicea. It provides the christological framework by means of which Athanasius eventually triumphed over the Arians. It is, however, also the structure of ideas which gave natural birth to Apollinarianism.

The principal difficulty faced by an Alexandrian christology has to do with the way it treats the human mind of Christ. If his mind is truly human then it is limited in a number of respects. If it is limited in its knowledge, then there are things that he in his humanity does not know, such as, the day of his return in glory. But this is surely an event of which God the Son, as omniscient, must be fully aware. This seems to imply that there are in Jesus Christ two quite different subjects, one who knows and one who does not know. But the possibility of speaking of two subjects in this way, the Word of God and Jesus the Man, was an anathema to the Alexandrians. It suggested a divided Christ, something wholly foreign to their way of thinking. They understood the incarnation as the act whereby the Word assumed human nature as his own. They were deeply suspicious that the expression 'the Word united a man to himself' indicated an unacceptable dualism. For them the human nature taken by the Word was real and complete but it was always his human nature, an aspect of his one being. Now if, as the Alexandrians assumed, the Word was the one subject of the incarnate life he must, for example, surely know the day of his own return in glory. But the Scriptures clearly indicate that he did not. It meant that although the Alexandrians formally affirmed that Christ had a human mind they found it difficult to account for its active role in Jesus life among us. But Jesus' untrammelled human agency as he struggled to overcome temptation and sought to live a life of obedience to God is precisely what the Gospel narratives appear to indicate.

The Antiochenes approached the matter from a quite different perspective. They formally acknowledged that salvation was an action of the divine Son bringing enlightenment and divinization to a darkened and corrupted human existence. But for them this was not the heart of the matter. Salvation was principally about Christ overcoming human disobedience and resolving the consequent estrangement of humanity from God. And this, they believed, could only be accomplished by the obedient life of a man, of one like ourselves. Theodore of Mopsuestia was perhaps the most eloquent exponent of Antiochene theology. R. A. Norris outlines his position:

The primary agent of man's redemption is God himself, acting in his eternal Son. Yet Theodore's understanding of human nature and of the human situation requires equally an act of man in the work of salvation. . . . [His] characteristic idea that man's redemption consists in the achievement of a free obedience to God demands that divine salvation be wrought not merely in man but through man. Human as well as divine action is requisite, not so much because it is man who is to be saved, as because the kind of salvation which is in question presupposes the free accord of the human will as one of its constituent elements. (*Manhood and Christ* p. 194)

The Antiochenes supported the Nicene Creed and vigorously defended the doctrine of the unchangeable nature of the divine Son. They were strongly opposed to Apollinarianism, but for rather different reasons to those of the Alexandrians. The Alexandrian argument that Christ has a human mind was based on their view that the act of incarnation was itself redemptive. Only the Word's assumption of a complete human nature, body and rational soul, could bring about our complete redemption. In an Antiochene soteriology the humanity of Christ was an active agent of our redemption, rather than merely its passive object. Consequently, the authentic exercise of Jesus' 'rational soul' was crucial for salvation. In his humanity Jesus thought, acted and grew in his knowledge and understanding of good and evil just as we do. He was consequently able to represent us in offering an acceptable obedience to God. It was a christological perspective that was able to take seriously the Gospel account of Jesus' human experiences, his temptations and his life of faith.

And this, as Theodore of Mopsuestia explains, was of utmost significance for their soteriology:

> If [the Man assumed] did not receive a soul, and if it was the Godhead that conquered sin, then what was effected can be of no possible advantage to us. The Lord's struggle would have been no more than gratification of the love of display.[12]

Theodore believed that if we are to take Christ's passion seriously we are compelled to affirm an active human agency in him. And it is this concern that lay at the heart of Antiochene christology. The principal difficulty it faced was how to explain the unity of Christ in the context of this duality of agency.

The Antiochenes were well aware of the need to affirm Christ's unity but they sought to express it in a way that did not either overwhelm his authentic human experience or undermine his full divinity. Thus, although Theodore was strongly opposed to any suggestion that there were in Christ two sons, the language he sometimes used can suggest that Christ is a compilation of two quite different persons. Consider a typical expression of his: 'Let us apply our minds to the distinction of natures; He who assumed is God and only-begotten Son, but the form of a slave, he who was assumed, is man.'[13] How did Theodore conceive the unity of these two disparate natures? One of his favourite images was that of indwelling. Jesus had spoken about his body as a temple that was to be destroyed. For Theodore the divine Son indwelt the temple of the man Jesus. He put him on as a garment:

> He united the whole man assumed with Himself, causing Him to share with Him in all the honours which He, the Son by nature indwelling him, enjoys. (*On the Incarnation* 7)[14]

In the incarnation the two natures came together in indissoluble unity as one *prosopon* or person. Person was here understood as the external presentation of a reality which might be twofold.[15] This *prosopon* is the proper subject of the activity of both divine and human natures. It is not a new *prosopon* formed by the union but is in fact the *prosopon* of the eternal Son.

Nevertheless, the Antiochenes were not finally successful in providing an adequate account of Christ's unity. *Prosopon*, the ground of the union, could be understood as an external representation, and the word 'conjunction' was generally used by them in preference to 'union' to describe the relation of the two natures. Often speaking of the relation as one of favour or grace the Antiochenes implied that the natures were held together by the Holy Spirit, an idea which suggested a form of Adoptionism. And this leads us to a question that an Antiochene christology always finds difficult to answer adequately. How was the relation of the divine and human in Christ qualitatively different from the indwelling of the Holy Spirit in a Christian? Antiochene theology, even at its best, was unable to provide a sufficiently strong conceptual base for Christ's unique being.

NESTORIUS (d.c. 451)

Alexandrian christology inevitably veers towards what might be called an incipient Apollinarianism, that is, the effective denial of an active human mind in Jesus. An Antiochene perspective, however, is always in danger of embracing a form of Nestorianism, that is, the view that Jesus Christ is some sort of conjunction of two quite distinct persons – the Word and the man Jesus.

What do we know of Nestorius? He was enthroned as patriarch of Constantinople in 428 and was soon to become notorious for propagating the heresy associated with his name. The irony is that there is little evidence that he was a true Nestorian in the way the word had been understood classically. He learned his theology from Theodore of Mopsuestia and his interpretation of Christ by and large followed that of his teacher summarized in the outline above. With little regard to the theological sensitivities of his opponents, one of Nestorius' early acts as patriarch was to challenge the appropriateness of the title *theotokos* used by the faithful when referring to Mary the mother of Jesus. In the Greek the expression suggests 'God-bearer' rather than 'Mother of God'. Nestorius would have preferred to describe her as the 'Christ-bearer'. Now it would be a mistake to think that he or any of those in the Antiochene school were at all hesitant about affirming the full deity of Christ. Their commitment to Nicene orthodoxy was never an issue with their opponents. The question for the Antiochenes was simply how one was to speak about the natures of Christ so as to safeguard both his unchangeable divinity and his full and active humanity. According to Nestorius the title *theotokos* should at least be supplemented by *anthropotokos*, the man-bearer. But his challenge to this traditional designation for Mary initiated an acrimonious debate with the Alexandrians and in particular with Cyril the patriarch of Alexandria. It was one that was only formally resolved in the synthesis achieved in the Chalcedonian Definition some two decades later.

To safeguard the authentic humanity of Christ, Nestorius argued that his two natures remained unaltered and distinct in the union. His unchangeable divinity was not reduced to the human, and his humanity was not overwhelmed by the divine Word. For this reason he preferred to speak of a conjunction rather than a union of these two objectively real natures. One can see why his theory left the impression of two persons being related to one another in a somewhat external way. Nestorius was, however, vigorously opposed to the idea that there were in Christ two quite different people:

> Christ is indivisible in his being Christ, but he is twofold in his being God and man. . . . We know not two Christs or two Sons or Only-begottens or Lords, not one and another Son, not a first and a second Christ, but one and the same, Who is seen in His created and increate natures. Quoted in J. N. D. Kelly Early Christian Doctrines, p. 314

But how then did he explain their union? Nestorius believed it was not a substantial or hypostatic union, neither was it a natural union. It was, rather, one of voluntary coalescence. Christ as presented to us in the Gospels was one *prosopon* considered as his outward aspect or form, resulting from the coming together of these two natures. Nestorius denied that the union was simply a harmony of his human and divine will or merely an act of God's favour. But he could never adequately explain why the relation between the natures was not something artificial or merely external. In contrast, Cyril his archopponent and Patriarch of Alexandria, was absolutely clear:

> If any one does not acknowledge that the Word which is from God the Father was personally [hypostatically] united with the flesh, and with his own flesh is one Christ, that is, one and the same God and man together, let him be anathema. If any one in the one Christ divides the persons [hypostasis] after their union, conjoining them with a mere conjunction in accordance with

worth, or a conjunction effected by authority or power, instead of a combination according to a union of natures, let him be anathema. (*The Twelve Anathemas of Cyril of Alexandria* 2 and 3) Documents of the Christian Church, second edition, selected and edited by Henry Bettenson (London, Oxford, New York, Oxford University Press, 1967) p. 46

For Cyril the two natures are united naturally in one subsisting reality or *hypostasis*. The Word is not changed or transformed in the incarnation. It remains what it was, existing eternally as God, yet in taking to itself the form of a servant something new is added.

THE *DEFINITION OF CHALCEDON*

To illuminate the difference between these two schools of thought it is helpful to consider how they treated the human mind of Christ. How, for instance, would they respond to the proposition that the Word of God had a human mind? Transposing the arguments from the *theotokos* debate we can construct their respective positions.

After the condemnation of Apollinarius the Alexandrians would have unreservedly accepted the above statement as true but remained silent in explaining how such a human mind actually operated. Whenever the Gospels suggested some limitation in Jesus' thought life, the Alexandrians were tempted in their exposition to sidestep the plain meaning of the text. The Antiochenes would have objected to the way the statement was formulated here. They would have preferred to speak of Jesus, the man or even the incarnate Christ having a human mind. They might have conceded that as a linguistic concession or communion of idioms we can refer such a mind to the Word, but strictly speaking the Word has a divine not a human mind. It is Jesus Christ, the Word incarnate who has a human mind. For them the expression would be in need of careful qualification.

It would be a mistake, however, to interpret the debate between these two parties as one of semantics or even as the ecclesial expression of power politics, although both of these were in plentiful supply during this contentious period. Rather, as we have seen, two quite different theories of salvation energizing their respective theologies had shaped these two distinct ways of understanding the person of Christ. And there was no obvious conceptual means at hand to bridge their distinct approaches.

However, in the rigour of the ongoing intellectual discussion among the leading protagonists, an awareness developed of the strengths of the opposing position and the need to make certain concessions. Eventually at the Council of Chalcedon in 451 a formula, based on the Symbol of Union,[16] was proposed which was able to include the positive elements of both perspectives and gain the formal assent of the majority of those present. Its foundation was the Alexandrian emphasis on the unity or integrity of Christ, the one who was truly God and truly man, whose two natures were united in one hypostasis. But it was also able to affirm clearly and unambiguously the Antiochene insight that Christ's divine and human natures each had their own integrity, authenticity and freedom of operation. Somehow in this formula the whole had become greater than its parts and the theology of the *Definition of Chalcedon* was able to offer to the Church a fuller and more comprehensive structure for the person of Jesus Christ than that of any of its participating theologians as

> . . . one and the same Christ, Son, Lord, Only-begotten, recognised in two natures, without confusion, without change, without division, without separation; the distinction of natures being in no way annulled by the union, but rather the characteristics of each nature being preserved and coming together to form one person [persona] and subsistence [hypostasis], not as parted or separated into two persons, but one and the same Son and Only-begotten God the Word, Lord Jesus Christ . . . (*Definition of Chalcedon*) Documents of the Christian Church, second edition, selected and edited by Henry Bettenson (London, Oxford, New York, Oxford University Press, 1967) pp. 51–52

In the incarnation the Word of God took to himself a human mind and body as his own, and that mind operated in an authentically human way – however difficult that might be for us to conceive.

CONCLUSION

After the Nicene settlement the Church's attention was drawn to the active humanity of Christ, in particular that of his human mind. Apollinarius' brilliant account of how such a mind was replaced in the incarnate Christ by the divine Word proved to be wholly unacceptable to the Church. The Alexandrian school affirmed that Christ had a human mind but their understanding of the Logos as the agent of the incarnate life meant that it was unable to attach any currency to this formal concession. The Antiochenes recognized both a divine and human agency in Christ but could not explain how his unity of person was anything more than an external presentation. They left themselves open to the charge that their christology implied the existence of two sons, divine and human, even though they vigorously denied it. In the ensuing debate the two sides became more aware of the strength of the opposing arguments and at the Council of Chalcedon the positive principles of each school were promulgated and received support from the majority of those present. Jesus Christ was one Son, one hypostasis or existing reality and his two natures were substantially united and not merely conjoined in this single existence. Yet his divine and human natures, although inseparable, were held to be neither mixed nor confused, but each maintained and so continued to operate according to its own distinct characteristics.

However, as we shall see, the activity of this human nature of Christ, particularly as it referred to his decision making, was an issue that Chalcedon had not settled to everyone's satisfaction.

CHAPTER FIVE

DIVINE AND HUMAN WILLING IN CHRIST

The Nicene Creed, receiving its final formulation at the Council of Constantinople in 381, shaped the Christian understanding of Jesus by interpreting the Gospel account of his incarnation, death, resurrection, ascension and final judgement of humankind as the redemptive mission of a person who is substantially one with God the Father. Afforded authoritative standing by the Church, and often the state, the Creed has acted as an interpretative lens through which the scriptural testimony to Jesus has been read and heard over the centuries. It has provided the basis for a trinitarian understanding of God, and consequently has served as the cornerstone of Christian theology. It has given rise to a range of theological and intellectual ideas in areas that lie far beyond those it was originally designed to resolve. One could say that it has functioned somewhat like a scientific theory. It offers a way of making sense of the complex raw material before it, that is, the biblical witness to the person of Christ and the Church's experience of his person in its life of worship and experience of salvation. And like all good theories it has been found to be illuminating in ways quite unforeseen by its original framers. Ecclesiastically, it has marked the boundaries of what the wider Church considers to be an acceptable interpretation of Jesus Christ. For well over a 1,000 years, until the radical critique of the Socinians in the late sixteenth century, the Nicene Creed's determinative role in Christian thought was never seriously challenged.

The *Definition of Chalcedon* was considered by its framers to be no more than an explanatory gloss on the authoritative Nicene text. It was a timely clarification of the nature of the incarnate Son's humanity and its relation to his divine being in the one person of Christ. It was held to be no more than an appendix to the principal narrative. What can we say of its role in shaping Christian thought? How effective has this particular formula been as a christological 'theory'?

The thrust of the argument in the previous chapter was that the *Definition of Chalcedon* was, in effect, a synthesis of two quite different christological models developed in the theological schools of Alexandria and Antioch, each shaped by its own particular theory of salvation. The Alexandrian focus was on the role of the divine Word as the subject of the incarnate life. His taking of human nature to himself in an act of humility was considered to be the central redemptive event. The Antiochene interest, on the other hand, was to safeguard both the unchangeable nature of the divine Word and the full and untrammelled expression of his humanity. The latter concern was crucial to their understanding of salvation for they deemed that it was as man that Christ freely chose to exercise the life of obedience to God that made possible our reconciliation. In short, the strength of the Alexandrian perspective was on the unity of Christ's person, that of the Antiochenes on the integrity of both his divine and human natures. The *Definition of Chalcedon* formally affirmed both.

Some commentators have argued that the difference between these two parties was no more than an unfortunate and unnecessary disagreement about words – that if there had been a little less heat in the debate and a little more freedom from political pressures the two theological schools might well have discovered they were, in effect, using different terminology to say much the same thing.[17] I don't think this is right. Such an argument fails to recognize the immense conceptual difficulties involved in integrating these two quite different christological models. The theory that the divine Logos is the subject of Christ's incarnate life does not easily account for Jesus' human experience of temptation and faith, his growth in knowledge and understanding, his need for prayer and his sense of estrangement from God. It is not surprising that the two parties found it difficult to accommodate each others point of view.

It was to be expected then that, in the aftermath of the Council, many Alexandrians found themselves deeply dissatisfied with its decisions. When news of the settlement reached the monks in Palestine and Egypt, they were enraged by what they viewed as its damaging concessions to an Antiochene dualism. Sensing that there had been a radical betrayal of the Nicene Creed they responded with anger and violence to the Definition. In Alexandria their murder of Patriarch Proterius led to the personal involvement of the emperor Marcian in the ongoing controversy. The Catholic historical theologian Aloys Grillmeier recognizes that in the emperor's response '[t]here is a political motive of course, for he sees that the well-being of the empire stands or falls with his responsibility for the unanimous acceptance of the formula of faith approved by the Council'.[18]As it turned out the emperor's worst fears were realized. Dissatisfaction with Chalcedon eventually led to the Non-Chalcedonian churches breaking away from the imperial church and their regions becoming dislocated from the political structure of what became known as the Byzantine Empire. These bodies, known under the general description of the Oriental Orthodox Churches, continue today as the Syrian Church of Antioch, the Syrian Church in India, the Coptic Church in Egypt, the Armenian Church and the Ethiopian Church. It is of interest that in recent years they have taken part in ecumenical discussions with the Eastern Orthodox Church in an attempt to resolve their longstanding disagreement over the *Definition of Chalcedon*.

Now the fact that the failure to integrate these two christological perspectives was able to divide an empire should alert us to the possibility that there is at the heart of this ongoing controversy a real theological issue at stake and not merely an inability of the parties to understand each other's terminology.

THE MONOPHYSITES

The Non-Chalcedonians were originally known as Monophysites for in opposition to the Definition they insisted that Christ had only one composite nature or *phusis*. Cyril of Alexandria, the renowned leader of the Alexandrian school, had used the expression 'the one nature, and that incarnate, of the divine Word' in the mistaken belief that it was sanctioned by Athanasius and was therefore orthodox. By nature Cyril meant a concrete individual. He did, however, recognize that there were two aspects, divinity and humanity, to Christ's being for which he employed a number of terms including 'manners of being', 'things' and even 'natures'. He was, consequently, able to subscribe with integrity to the 'two nature' formulation in the Symbol of Union (433) which shaped the Chalcedonian Definition.

But Cyril's followers and successors were highly suspicious of his concessions to the Antiochene position. They were insistent that the incarnate Christ had a single composite nature in a sense that precluded a Chalcedonian interpretation. Their theory, as it was promulgated first by an enthusiastic and somewhat muddled Alexandrian named Eutyches and then by the Non-Chalcedonians, was viewed by the orthodox community as a regressive step in the christological discussion. It indicated a return to a simpler, more Apollinarian way of conceiving of Christ. The Monophysites dealt with the perennial paradox that Jesus was both true God and true Man, by postulating in Christ a unity of being and action which invariably neglected or undermined his active human reality. The theology of the Monophysites ranged from that of Severus, Patriarch of Antioch (512–518), whose christology was comparatively close to that of Cyril, to an extreme form which was difficult to distinguish from a thoroughgoing Doceticism (the view that Christ only appeared to be human). Whatever distinctions were to emerge among the Monophysites in their internal debates, they were of one mind in their determined opposition to the teaching of Chalcedon. They could not reconcile their perception of Christ to the Definition's proposal that he was 'to be acknowledged in two natures, without confusion, without change, without division, without separation; the distinction of natures being in no way abolished because of the union, but rather the characteristic property of each nature being preserved . . .' Why were they so implacably opposed to this formulation?

The Monophysites were unable to conceive how there could be in the one person of Christ two distinct principles of action. They believed that there was just one operation, one new divine–human energy or *theandric* action in Christ's incarnate life. By this they meant not two harmonious actions working in concert, but rather one indivisible principle of activity. Pseudo-Dionysius the Areopagite first formulated the theory of this united action:

> . . . not having done things Divine as God, nor things human as man, but exercising for us a certain new God-incarnate energy of God having become man. (*Fourth letter*) The Works of Dionysius the Areopagite, translated by John Parker (London and Oxford, 1897), p. 143

The Monophysites changed the word 'new' to 'single' and the expression 'one theandric energy' encapsulated the essence of their difference with the Chalcedonians. To their minds the Definition rightly affirmed that the being of Christ was only one hypostasis, one person, one Son. But alongside this Chalcedon indicated that his activity was twofold – that there were in him two distinct, albeit harmonious, principles of operation, divine and human, each acting according to its own particular characteristics. And Non-Chalcedonians were implacably opposed to the apparently dualistic implications of this view of Christ.

The difficulty, however, with the argument that there is in Christ a single energy or mode of operation becomes apparent when an explanation is offered of the nature of that sole operation. If it is divine, then Christ only appears to act as a human, every one of his actions is simply that of God using the human body as an instrument. On the other hand, if all his activity is simply human then there is no reason to consider him as the incarnation of a divine being. And so it was proposed by them that Christ's activity was of a unique sort. It is *theandric*, that is, it is a single composite divine–human action flowing from one composite nature. But a hybrid action such as this indicates a hybrid person, an amalgam, sometimes referred to as a *tertium quid*, one who in his being and action is neither truly God nor truly man, and who is, consequently, soteriologically inadequate on both counts. The inherent difficulties of the theory of a single energy in Christ were further highlighted when the discussion turned to the nature of his will.

MONOTHELITISM

The theory that Christ had only one will was formally introduced by the Emperor Heraclius as a compromise formulation in order to restore the Monophysites to communion with the imperial Chalcedonian Church. This was considered to be strategically important in the face of the Islamic threat to Egypt when the greater part of that country was Monophysite and so in danger of being dislocated not only religiously but also politically from Constantinople. The '*Ecthesis*' (638), as the document drawn up by Sergius, Patriarch of Constantinople, was known, forbids the mention of one or two energies in Christ and asserts that the two natures of Christ were united in a single will. Such a formulation had immediate appeal to many Monophysites who believed that an affirmation of a unity of intention or will in Christ adequately compensated for the dualistic tendency of the two natures doctrine that they discerned in the *Definition of Chalcedon*. Through it a number of those who had been estranged were reconciled with the imperial Church.

For some 40 or so years this view that there was in Christ just one will was officially sanctioned by Church and State. Superficially it appears to be not merely non-contentious but intuitively obvious. On closer examination, however, it takes us right to the heart of the christological problem. The Church had long since agreed that Jesus possessed a human mind and formally rejected the arguments of Apollinarius that his mental activity was simply that of the divine Logos. Jesus was like us not only physically but also psychologically. He had a physical body and a rational human soul or mind. On the other hand, as the incarnation of the eternal Son of God, it was taken for granted that Jesus also had a divine mind. How then were the Chalcedonian proponents of the two nature theory of Christ, including Pope Honorius, able to support the idea that there was in him only one will?

The essence of their argument seems to have been that there is a distinction between the operation of the mind in each nature and the specific act of willing which lies not in the natures but in the hypostasis or person of Christ. The will is therefore understood by them to be external to the natures. It is the ultimate operator of all the actions performed by them. As the person or hypostasis is single so also there is only one will. Such a theory avoided the possibility of a serious internal discord within Christ implied by the argument that he had two wills.

Maximus the Confessor (580–662) was the principle defender of Chalcedonian orthodoxy. His response to Monothelitism was founded on the *Definition of Chalcedon*'s affirmation that Jesus was in his humanity like us in all respects, apart from sin. He argued that one of the determining characteristics of human existence is our 'free self-determining action' (*kinesis autoexousias*). To act in a human way means to be able to choose without external compulsion. If Jesus is truly man he must will as a human. If he is truly God he must exercise a divine will. The will cannot simply be dislocated from the nature as if it were an external or unrelated faculty. Maximus believed that the possibility of any internal discord in Jesus' actions was removed once we recognize the sinless nature of his human existence. For in his person the human will conforms voluntarily to that of the divine. This short summary does scant justice to the richness of Maximus' anthropology and his careful distinction between a free (gnomic) will and a natural will as part of his comprehensive response to the Monothelites. He was without doubt the outstanding theologian of the period.

Although Maximus' theology was condemned before a council in Constantinople in 662, where he lost both his right hand and his tongue in punishment for his teaching, within two decades the Sixth Ecumenical Council of 681 reversed their decision and recognized as orthodox the view that Christ has two wills.

YOUR WILL BE DONE

Modern readers may well find this discussion about two wills in Christ to be rather technical and somewhat removed from the naturalness and power of the Gospel story. To test the relevance or interpretive value of the *Definition of Chalcedon* let us leave the historical survey for a moment and consider briefly the significance of the prayer of Jesus in the Garden of Gethsemane. In the Gospel of Matthew it takes this form:

> Going a little farther, he fell with his face to the ground and prayed, 'My Father, if it is possible, may this cup be taken from me. Yet not as I will, but as you will.' . . . He went away a second time and prayed, 'My Father, if it is not possible for this cup to be taken away unless I drink it, may your will be done.' (Mt. 26.39,42)

How was this prayer interpreted theologically by the New Testament authors? All three Synoptic writers highlight the details of the incident in their account of the passion. It has its place in the unfolding drama of that last week as the final step of Jesus' freely chosen journey of obedience towards Jerusalem and so to an impending death. In each of the three Gospels it is clear that his decision to choose the will of the Father rather than his own natural inclination is a moment of deep significance in the unfolding Easter story. The Synoptic Gospels imply that the meaning of the passion is to be understood, at least in part, in terms of Jesus' personal act of obedience to God.

In Paul's writing we find three somewhat different perspectives on the willing subject of the decision made at Gethsemane. First, he interprets it as an act of human volition:

> Consequently, just as the result of one trespass was condemnation for all men, so also the result of one act of righteousness was justification that brings life for all men. For just as through the disobedience of the one man the many were made sinners, so also

through the obedience of the one man the many will be made righteous. (Rom. 5.18,19)

According to Paul, Jesus' single act of human obedience undoes the estrangement and resulting havoc brought to the world by the first Adam's act of disobedience and leads to righteousness and life for the many. This idea of a human act of faithfulness undoing the wrong brought about by our human parents was famously developed by Irenaeus of Lyons in his theory of recapitulation and later in Reformed soteriology as the doctrine of Jesus' active obedience.

Second, it is for Paul an act of divine condescension by the eternal Son

> [w]ho, being in very nature God, did not count equality with God something to be grasped, but made himself nothing, taking the very nature of a servant, being made in human likeness. And being found in human appearance as a man, he humbled himself and became obedient to death – even death on a cross! (Phil. 2.6–8)

Using what might well be a hymn already known in the early churches, Paul encourages Christians to have the same attitude as the one who took human form and chose to die as a man. The one willing to take this path was one who could be spoken of as 'being in the very nature of God'. The decision at Gethsemane was then the historical unfolding of the willing act of the divine Son made in eternity.

Third, it was the outworking of the free act of God the Father's volition as he demonstrated his love for the world:

> Very rarely will anyone die for a righteous man, though for a good man someone might possibly dare to die. But God demonstrates his own love for us in this: While we were yet sinners Christ died for us. (Rom. 5.7,8)

The death of the Son is the Father's decision to love and redeem an alien and lost world. If he has freely given his own Son he will surely do all else that is required for the salvation of his people. Christ's death is the loving act of the Father. Now Monothelitism is clearly ill-equipped to hold together these varied perspectives and so offer a coherent account of volitional agency with respect to Jesus' death. But such an account is essential for our understanding of the atonement. Monothelites have always been embarrassed by the expression 'not my will but yours' and struggled to explain the significance of the spiritual battle that Jesus entered into during his time of prayer at Gethsemane.

How, then, are the credal formulae of Nicea and Chalcedon able to help us to interpret these significant texts in a more coherent way? As a 'theological theory' Nicea implies that, on account of their substantial unity, the divine willing of Father and Son is ultimately one undivided action. The choice of God the Son to humble himself and taste death on the cross as a man is not to be distinguished from the decision of the Father to give over his Son to death out of his love for the world. The personal subjects are distinct, yet the content of their decision is one. There is ultimately no division in the mind or being of the Triune God either at Gethsemane or Golgatha, even though all three divine persons play distinct roles in the dynamic of the redemptive drama.

Further, Chalcedon's doctrine of two natures indicates that there is in Christ both a human and a divine willing. Jesus' decision to submit to God's purpose at Gethsemane and to resist the temptation to turn aside from the road to Jerusalem is in principle the same form of temptation that we each face in our calling to a life of obedience. He prays as we might in such circumstances because he needs the spiritual assistance of God so that he might choose well. But the person who in his human nature seeks through prayer to obey God at Gethsemane is the same person, who in his divinity, chose before the ages to take the form of a servant and die as a man in order that men and women might now live. Nicea helps us to see how the atonement is both the loving act of God the Father and also the faithful action of the incarnate Son. Chalcedon provides a framework by which we are able to recognize the efficacy of Christ's atoning action as dependent on both his divine submission to a human death and his human act of obedience towards God.

THE SUBJECT OF THE TWO NATURES IN CHRIST

In what sense can we speak of a single subject in the person of Christ if in his one reality there are two distinct natures and consequently both a divine and a human willing?

In his book, *The Orthodox Faith*, John of Damascus (c. 675–c. 749) brilliantly summarized and clarified the theology of the Greek

Fathers and so signalled the end of this fascinating, though turbulent, age of christological reflection. In dealing with the question of willing in Christ he made some important logical distinctions about the nature of personal action or energy:

> But observe that energy and capacity for energy, and the product of energy, and the agent of energy, are all different. Energy is the efficient [*drastike*] and essential activity of nature: the capacity for energy is the nature from which proceeds energy: the product of energy is that which is effected by energy: and the agent of energy is the person or subsistence which uses the energy. (III 15) NPNF 2nd IX, p. 60

Transposing this fairly complex analysis into language with which we might be a little more comfortable we could say

a. there is the subject of the action which is the person;
b. there is the capacity for action which is the nature of the person;
c. there is the activity itself, which is an operation of one of the natures;
d. there is the resultant act, which is always to be referred back to the subject or person.

All of Christ's activities are thus the actions of the person or hypostasis of the incarnate Christ. They are always performed through either his divine or human nature. The person dies on the cross but he does so in and through his physical body. His death is redemptive because the person who dies is, in his divinity, the eternal Son of God, and in his humanity he is one who fully shares in our condition. Likewise, to the one metaphysical subject or person is attributed both the eternal divine decision to take human form and suffer death as a man, and the human willingness in Gethsemane to submit to the purpose of God. The person is one and inseparable. The capacity to will, however, is distinguishable according to the natures.

CONCLUSION

At the beginning of the chapter, a question was asked about the effectiveness of the *Definition of Chalcedon* as a Christian interpretive theory. How illuminating is it as an interpretative tool when considering the biblical testimony to Jesus Christ and the Church's experience of worship and salvation?

First, from the discussion above it is apparent that the Definition played a critical role in illuminating the deficiencies of Monothelitism as a christological model. In contrast it provided a way of interpreting the volitional agency in Christ which was able to take seriously both the Gospel witness to Jesus' prayer at Gethsemane and also the Church's liturgical affirmation of the divine act of condescension by the eternal Son.

Second, it allowed Christ's redemptive work to be interpreted as a human act towards God. The interdependence of soteriology and christology means that the value of any theory of Christ's person can be tested with respect to the views of salvation that it generated. Assuming that the work of John of Damascus provides a synopsis of the best of Greek theology we ask: 'how faithful was he in interpreting the scriptural witness to Christ's saving action?' In particular, was he able to maintain the biblical emphasis of Jesus' saving work as that of a human representing our race before God which was the genius of the Antiochene perspective? Was Jesus' humanity redemptively significant? Showing himself remarkably free from the Athanasian view that salvation was effected principally by the divine power of the Word of God, John argues:

> . . . in that when man was overcome He did not make another victorious over the tyrant, not did he snatch man by might from death, but in His goodness and justice He made him, who had become through his sins the slave of death, himself once more conqueror and rescued like by like, most difficult though it seemed . . . (*The Orthodox Faith* III 1) NPNF 2nd IX, p. 45

> And he becomes obedient to the Father Who is like unto us, and finds a remedy for our disobedience in what He had assumed from us, and became a pattern of obedience to us without which it is not possible to obtain salvation. (III 1) NPNF 2nd IX, p. 46

It demonstrates God's justice that it was a man who overcame the tyrant and it was a man who in obedience to the Father secured our eternal salvation. Chalcedon clearly was able to preserve an interpretative insight which emphasized the redemptive significance of Christ's humanity – a theme close to the heart of a number of

New Testament authors. It was a perspective of which the leading theologians of the age immediately prior to Chalcedon had almost completely lost sight.

Third, Chalcedon's insistence that each nature continued to operate according to its essential characteristics allowed the Gospel narrative of Jesus' life to be read as one of human development, of growth in wisdom and grace, of human temptation and faith and finally of a sense of estrangement from the presence of God in the hour of death. John of Damascus successfully upheld the doctrine of the two natures of Christ in the face of an articulate Monophysitism. But at the end of the day, having triumphed technically, he so qualified the freedom of Christ's human willing, and the limitations of his human knowing that there was little left of Jesus' human agency. The Jesus he describes appears to be quite different from the one put forward by the Gospels. Consider how John struggles to accommodate the idea that Jesus prayed for himself:

> For His holy mind was in no need either of any uprising towards God, since it had been once and for all united in subsistence with the God Word, or of any petitioning of God. (III 24) NPNF 2nd IX, p. 70

> [I]s it not clear to all that He said this as a lesson to us to ask help in our trials only from God, and to prefer God's will to our own, and as a proof that he did actually appropriate to himself the attributes of our nature. (III 24) NPNF 2nd IX, p. 71

Although serving the Church as the great champion of Chalcedon, John of Damascus could not allow that Jesus grew in wisdom and grace, needed to pray or was either ignorant or fearful. Why was this? Why was the *Definition of Chalcedon* unable to preserve these basic New Testament insights even among its most eloquent of supporters? Was there something of theological significance missing in this christological theory?

CHAPTER SIX

JESUS AND THE SPIRIT

The Church chose a particular biblical narrative as the master-story or interpretive key to understand the person of Christ. It is encapsulated in the phrase: 'the Word became flesh.' Through its ecumenical creeds and christological formulae it sought to articulate what is implied by this foundational concept. Positively, these formulations are key elements in a process of imaginative theological construction, a movement towards greater precision and clarity, not only about the person of Jesus but also about the manner of God's being. Defensively, they are part of a protective strategy designed to safeguard an incarnational understanding of Christ from distortion by clarifying the boundaries of acceptable interpretation. This framework of ideas, both creative and protective, evolved in stages through a complex process of development and shaping. For seven centuries many of the best minds of the Church, deeply influenced by their reading of the scriptures, engaged in a learned, imaginative and passionate debate as they sought to ensure that the officially sanctioned account of Jesus did full justice to the Gospel story. The broadly agreed christological settlement that was eventually achieved within the Church at the close of this formative period was ably summarized in the writings of John of Damascus. The shape and content of this understanding were determined primarily by the Nicene Creed, formalized at Constantinople in 381, and to a lesser extent by the *Definition of Chalcedon* promulgated in 451. These, we might say, were the principal tools used by the Church to promulgate, explain and defend the good news that for our salvation the Son of God became as we are.

What do we make of the christology that emerged from this long process of construction? Was it fit for purpose? Did it offer an adequate account of the person of Jesus as he is portrayed in the Scriptures and encountered in the worship of the Church?

At the end of Chapter Five we indicated that the christology of John of Damascus, and so by implication the greater part of the Church of his time, struggled to concede Jesus' human dependence on God, his need to pray for himself and his reliance on divine grace. Why was this? Chalcedon had promulgated the dogma that the divine and human natures of Christ were not to be confused but rather that each manifest its own distinct characteristics. John had ably defended this position and gone on to champion the view that there is in the one person of Christ both a divine and a human willing. The theological structure was firmly in place to affirm that Jesus in his humanity, like that of humankind in general was totally dependent on divine grace. But John chose not to take this path. When considering the issue he opted rather to employ an argument that effectively undermined the Chalcedonian principle outlined above:

> For if in truth the flesh was united with God the Word from its first origin, or rather if it existed in Him and was identical in subsistence with Him, how was it that it was not endowed completely with all wisdom and grace? (*The Orthodox Faith* III 21) NPNF 2nd IX, p. 69

The incarnation is here taken to mean that the human nature of Christ was spiritually perfected at conception and therefore in no ongoing need of divine grace. The problem with such an argument is that it flies in the face of the biblical testimony. The Gospel narrative of Jesus is that of a man always dependent on divine grace as it is mediated through the Holy Spirit. And the inability to recognize and affirm this perspective clearly is a significant weakness of John's christology and so it would seem of the ancient church.

To appreciate the force of this charge it might be of value to summarize briefly the scriptural witness to the work of the Holy Spirit in the person of Jesus.

THE BIBLICAL TESTIMONY

The Scriptures have much to say of the agency of the Holy Spirit, or the grace of God, in the life of Jesus. Here is an outline of some aspects of his empowering activity as they are found in the New Testament.

First, the body of Christ is held to be miraculously formed in the womb of Mary through the direct action of the Holy Spirit: '[A]n angel of the Lord appeared to him in a dream and said, "Joseph son of David, do not be afraid to take Mary home as your wife, because what is conceived in her is from the Holy Spirit"' (Mt. 1.20).

Second, the boy Jesus is viewed as developing in stature, wisdom and knowledge as the grace of God rested upon his life: 'And the child grew and became strong; he was filled with wisdom, and the grace of God was upon him. . . . And Jesus grew in wisdom and stature, and in favour with God and men' (Lk. 2.40,52).

Third, the public ministry of Jesus is inaugurated as the Holy Spirit descended upon him at his baptism in the Jordan. From this time he was considered to be 'full of the Holy Spirit' (Lk. 4.1). 'As soon as Jesus was baptized, he went up out of the water. At that moment heaven was opened, and he saw the Spirit of God descending like a dove and lighting upon him' (Mt. 3.16).

Fourth, through the Holy Spirit Jesus is equipped with the extraordinary powers and gifts necessary for his ministry. The outstanding witness to this empowering is the prophecy from Isaiah which was read publicly by Jesus in his home town and applied by him to his own mission: 'The Spirit of the Sovereign Lord is on me, because the Lord has anointed me to preach good news to the poor' (Is. 61.1). Peter's sermon at Pentecost as recorded in the Acts of the Apostles indicates that Jesus is enabled by God to perform the miracles which confirm and attest his ministry: 'Jesus of Nazareth, a man approved of God by miracles and wonders and signs, which God did by him' (Acts 2.22). That the miracles in Jesus' ministry should be ascribed to the Holy Spirit receives additional support from the Gospel accounts of his exorcisms. Luke's Gospel indicates that Jesus casts out devils by the 'finger of God', that is, by the infinite power of God. The parallel account in Matthew refers the exorcisms directly to the Spirit of God: 'But if I drive out demons by the Spirit of God, then the kingdom of God has come upon you' (Mt. 12.28).

Fifth, the Spirit guided, directed, comforted and supported Jesus in the whole course of his ministry, temptations, obedience and sufferings. He was led by the Spirit into the wilderness (Mt. 4.1); by his assistance he stood firm throughout the temptations and he was empowered by him in his preaching (Lk. 4.14).

Sixth, Jesus' sacrificial self-offering is dependent on the enabling of the Holy Spirit: 'How much more, then, will the blood of Christ, who through the eternal Spirit offered himself unblemished to God, cleanse our consciences from acts that lead to death? (Heb. 9.14)

Seventh, although the resurrection of Jesus is understood in the Scriptures to be the concerted work of the three triune persons, the immediate efficacy of the action is ascribed to the Holy Spirit: 'And if the Spirit of him who raised Jesus from the dead is living in you, he who raised Christ from the dead will also give life to your mortal bodies through his Spirit' (Rom. 8.11).

We see then that from conception to resurrection the scriptural narrative of Jesus' life is that of a man formed, empowered, guided, comforted and ultimately raised from the dead by the Holy Spirit. This dependency of Jesus on the Spirit of God was a perspective largely absent from the orthodox theology of the Early Church and completely missing from that of John of Damascus. There were, however, some notable exceptions to this oversight among the Church Fathers.

IRENAEUS AND THEODORE

Irenaeus, Bishop of Lyons, a profound biblical theologian, recognized that Jesus in his humanity was dependent on the empowering action of the Holy Spirit for his prophetic ministry. 'For inasmuch as the Word of God was man from the root of Jesse, and son of Abraham, in this respect did the Spirit of God rest upon Him, and anoint Him to preach the gospel to the lowly.'[19] He argued further that from the fullness or overflow of Jesus' own experience of the Holy Spirit we ourselves were to be blessed.

> Therefore did the Spirit of God descend upon Him, [the Spirit] of Him who has promised by the prophets that he would anoint Him, so that we, receiving from the abundance of His unction, might be saved. (*Against Heresies* 3.9.3) ANF I, p. 423

This idea of Jesus' dependence on God is also apparent in a complex but significant passage emphasizing the weakness of Jesus' humanity and the healing ministry of the Holy Spirit. Irenaeus' argument seems to be that the divine image is renewed in the man Jesus through the Spirit so that in due course it may be restored in our lives.

> ' . . . the Lord commending to the Holy Spirit His own man, who had fallen among thieves, whom He Himself compassionated, and bound up his wounds, giving two royal *denaria*; so that we, receiving by the Spirit the image and superscription of the Father and the Son might cause the *denarium* to be fruitful . . .'[20]

Over the next 200 years almost nothing was said of the relation of the Spirit to Jesus' human life in orthodox theology. There are a number of reasons for this. First, until the work of Basil of Caesarea at the end of the fourth century, almost no attention was paid to pneumatological questions and it was difficult for many theologians to conceptualize the Holy Spirit as an independent agent active in Christ's life. Second, the debate with the Arians, outlined in Chapter Three, made orthodox theologians particularly sensitive to any suggestion that Jesus might be dependent on the Spirit. Their commitment to the '*homoousion*', the doctrine that the Son was of one substance with the Father, meant that they were unwilling to support a theory which seemed to imply that he was in some way subordinate to God. Third, the idea of Jesus' dependence on the Spirit was already tainted by its surface link with Adoptionism, the heresy that Jesus was only adopted into divine sonship when the Spirit came upon him at his baptism.

However, the recognition that Jesus possessed a human mind, universally conceded after the defeat of Apollinarianism, compelled the Church to think more seriously about the nature of his humanity. For Theodore of Mopsuestia this was far more than the formal acknowledgement of the presence of a human soul in Jesus. It was, rather, an affirmation that the experiences of Jesus were themselves truly human:

> But suppose, as you would have it, that the Deity took the role of consciousness in him who was assumed. How was he affected with fear in his suffering? Why, in the face of immediate need, did he stand in want of vehement prayers – prayers which, as the blessed Paul says, he brought before God with a loud and clamorous voice and with many tears?[21]

So clear an understanding of Jesus' emotional and spiritual pain leads Theodore to the recognition that Jesus is dependent on the strengthening power of God's Spirit:

> The man who was thus assumed by the Word . . . received in himself the grace of the Spirit in its entirety, while to other men he gave a portion of that which was his in its fullness. . . . It was this man . . . and not the Divine Word, that needed the Spirit to justify him, to enable him to overcome Satan and work miracles, to teach him what he should do; and for all these purposes he received the indwelling of the Spirit at his baptism.[22]

Jesus, the man assumed by the Word, receives the Spirit without measure, while all others experience only a portion of his fullness. The Spirit empowers Jesus to confront evil and do mighty works; it guides him and sanctifies his life. Theodore argues that Jesus' holy life is itself the fruit of the Spirit's enabling work, arguing that he 'was always without stain by the power of the Holy Spirit'.[23] In his exposition of Jn 1.16, Theodore explains how the work of the Spirit in the life of Jesus is significant for our salvation:

> Of his fullness, he says, we have all received – that is to say, it is of his abundance that we receive the grace of the Spirit which we are given. . . . For through union with God the Word, by the mediation of the Spirit, he has become sharer in the true Sonship. We receive a part of his spiritual grace, and through this same (grace) we are made participants with him of adoptive sonship, although we are far away from this honour.[24]

What Jesus has received through the Spirit, we ourselves receive by our participation in him.

Both in the theology of Irenaeus and that of Theodore, along with some of his fellow Antiochenes, we find a clear doctrine of the Spirit empowering the dependent humanity of Christ with an anointing which is deemed to be significant for our own salvation. Such an understanding is, however, exceptional among the Fathers. Although Chalcedon promulgated the view that the human nature of Christ operated according to it own natural characteristics, and John of Damascus ably championed it, in practice such a perspective was undermined by a tendency to hold that the divine nature dominated the human. This was achieved through a realistic application of the *communicatio idiomata*, the linguistic device whereby attributes of one nature are applied to the other. It was almost universally held in the Church in the centuries immediately after Chalcedon that Jesus did not need to pray or receive divine assistance in his own person. He did not require empowerment by the Holy Spirit:

> 'It is evident enough,' says Dorner, 'that the Christological result thus arrived at by the ancient Church . . . was far from bringing the matter to a close. The human nature of Christ was curtailed in that, after the manner of Apollinaris, the head of the Divine hypostasis was set upon the trunk of human nature, and the unity of the person thus preserved at the cost of the humanity'. [25]

Despite the creeds and the work of those who championed them, the christology of the Church had by and large reverted to a subtle form of Apollinarianism.

A FRESH FOCUS ON PNEUMATOLOGY

The general shape and characteristics of the christology of the ancient Church, encapsulated in the work of John of Damascus, experienced no significant development or challenge until the sixteenth century. During most of this period the focus of theology had moved away from questions of christology, which were considered to have been settled decisively, to a new range of issues, particularly those relating to salvation. The nature of free will, grace, faith, satisfaction and divine righteousness were among the matters that most occupied Christian minds through the Middle Ages on into the Reformation period. The attentiveness to questions of salvation, however, led eventually to a renewed interest in the work of the Holy Spirit. John Calvin one of the three leading teachers of the Magisterial Reformation came to be known as the theologian of the Holy Spirit:

> The fundamental interest of Calvin as a theologian lay, it is clear, in the region broadly designated soteriological. Perhaps we may go further and add that, within this broad field, his interest was most intense in the application to the sinful soul of the salvation wrought out by Christ, – in a word in what is technically known as the *ordo salutis*. This has even been made his reproach in some

quarters, and we have been told that the main fault of the Institutes as a treatise in theological science lies in its too subjective character. Its effect, at all events, has been to constitute Calvin pre-eminently the theologian of the Holy Spirit. (Benjamin B Warfield, *John Calvin the Theologian* (Presbyterian Board of Education 1909))

The third book of Calvin's *Institutes of the Christian Religion* was subtitled: 'The mode of obtaining the grace of Christ, the benefits it confers, and the effects resulting from it.' It is in effect a systematic pneumatology, an extended exposition of the Spirit's ministry in the justification, sanctification and glorification of the Church.

In the sixteenth century 'the Spirit' consequently became for many far more than a doctrinal concept or liturgical expression. It was associated directly with their own experience of salvation, their joy in worship and the spiritual vitality of their prayer and service to God. In sections of the Radical Reformation, most notoriously among the Zwickau Prophets and the Munster Anabaptists, it also became linked with supernatural religious phenomena, in particular with prophetic utterance and divine guidance. In seventeenth-century England the Quakers came to understand the Spirit in terms of the directness of divine revelation. Christ was understood to make himself known to the individual worshipper immediately through the 'inner light'.

Yet in all of this, the activity of the Spirit, although now theologically basic to the doctrine of salvation and of primary existential importance to the believing community, was not applied to its interpretation of Christ. Christians did not relate their own experience of the Spirit or their theology of salvation to their understanding of how Jesus himself was empowered.

Possibly the most articulate attempt since the Church Fathers to integrate theologically the saving work of the Spirit in the believer with the doctrine of Christ's person was that of the seventeenth-century British theologian, John Owen. He was a man of immense learning, steeped in the christology of the Early Church and shaped by the soteriology of the Reformers. In his important study, *Discourse on the Holy Spirit* he includes a careful consideration of the work of the Holy Spirit in the life of Jesus. And he does so within the framework of a classical christology determined by Nicea and Chalcedon.

THE CHRISTOLOGY OF JOHN OWEN

John Owen related the soteriological insights of the Reformation, particularly its emphasis on the agency of the Spirit in recreating the truly human, to his interpretation of the person of Christ. He argued that the primary work of the Spirit in the work of the Gospel or new creation is to restore the image of God in the Church. And the foundation and prototype of this wider restorative work is the renewal of the divine image in the humanity of Christ. In short, it was his thesis that the work which the Spirit was to accomplish in Christ's mystical body, he must first bring to completion in Christ's physical body:

> God, in the human nature of Christ, did perfectly renew that blessed image of his in our nature which we lost in Adam, with an addition of many glorious endowments which Adam was not made partaker of. . . . God designed and gave unto Christ grace and glory; and he did it that he might be the prototype of what he designed unto us, and would bestow upon us.[26]

The human life of Christ is for Owen a paradigm for our own renewed existence. The sanctifying of his human nature is not only the model but also the foundation of our own sanctification. Owen's awareness of the frailty of Jesus' humanity apart from the Spirit and his emphasis on the divine forming that took place in Jesus' life throws fresh light on some otherwise difficult texts:

> In bringing many sons and daughters to glory, it was fitting that God, for whom and through whom everything exists, should make the pioneer of their salvation perfect through what he suffered. Both the one who makes people holy and those who are made holy are of the same family. (Heb. 2.10,11)

> During the days of Jesus' life on earth, he offered up prayers and petitions with loud cries and tears to the one who could save him from death, and he was heard because of his reverent submission. Although he was a son, he learned obedience from what he suffered and, once made perfect, he became the source of eternal salvation for all who obey him. (Heb. 5.7–9)

Owen understood the incarnation to mean that the Son not only took upon himself a human nature but also entered fully into the human condition as we now find it:

His calling us brethren, and owning of us, made him instantly obnoxious unto all the miseries the guilt whereof we had contracted upon ourselves. The owning of the alliance unto us cost him, as it were all he was worth; for being rich, 'for our sakes he became poor.' He came into the prison and into the furnace to own us.[27]

He was born into our world of compromise and corruption, experiencing its joys, its pain and suffering, not as an outsider free from its seductive influence, but tempted in every way as we are. He lived before God as we do, dependent on the Spirit's guidance, comfort and empowering. He rose early in the morning to pray because he was in dire need of God's help. He sought to obey God and live in the light of his will, obedient to his particular calling. He knew the darkness and desolation of one who has experienced separation from the Father.

Owen's christology is a robust exposition of the Antiochene element of Chalcedonian orthodoxy – that each nature preserves its own characteristic properties. Christ's human nature is not overpowered by divinity, but flourishes according to its own principles – it is 'autokinetic'. But Owen was also a vigorous proponent of the Alexandrian emphasis on Christ's unity. Jesus Christ is, for him, the incarnation of the eternal Son, the one who humbled himself by taking to himself a human body and soul:

> . . . the Son of God becoming in time what he was not, the Son of man, ceased not thereby to be what he was, even the eternal Son of God.[28]

Using the analysis of personal agency developed by John of Damascus, Owen held that the incarnate Christ is the single subject of all the actions performed through both his natures:

> [W]hatever he doth in and about our salvation, it is done by that one person, God and man. . . . Whatever acts are ascribed unto him, however immediately performed, in or by the human nature, or in and by his divine nature, they are all acts of that one person, in whom are both these natures.[29]

In all this Owen is little more that a faithful expositor of classical christology. The significant new insight that Owen brought to this discussion had to do with the relation between the natures of Christ. He argued that although the human and divine natures were hypostatically united in one subsistence, in matters of agency the divine nature acted on the human not directly but through the Spirit:

> The Holy Spirit is the Spirit of the Son, no less than the Spirit of the Father. . . . And hence is he the immediate operator of all divine acts of the Son himself, even on his own human nature . . .[30]

The Logos does not replace the human mind in Jesus or overpower its free action. Rather he leads and guides it through the Spirit. In his humanity Jesus is as we are. He knows and responds to God as we do – by the agency of the Spirit.

CONCLUSION

Owen showed how a christology faithful to Chalcedon was nevertheless able to affirm Jesus as one who was filled and empowered by the Holy Spirit, a person wholly dependent on God. He was able to safeguard a view of Christ's humanity as the model or paradigm of our own Christian lives, and the person of Christ as truly one of us standing on our behalf in the presence of the Father.

Such a perspective allows the Gospel account of Jesus' life to be taken with greater seriousness than had generally been afforded it by the tradition. Jesus prayed because he was in need. He learnt obedience through the sufferings of life. He was continually guided and comforted by the Spirit. He grew in wisdom and understanding as any Jewish youngster might, learning from the Scriptures at the local synagogue. He was a Jew influenced and shaped by the hopes of Second Temple Judaism, in the context of Roman imperialistic power and the allure of a sophisticated Greek culture. He was a man of deep spirituality, who became aware not only of his particular mission before God, but of his unique relation with the Father and so of his peculiar authority. By faith he knew he was the true Son of God beloved of the Father.

This brief outline of John Owen's christology along with that of Irenaeus and Theodore of Mopsuestia has been introduced into the discussion to indicate how a classical christology has within itself the resources to affirm vigorously that Jesus as he lived and ministered among us was wholly dependent on God. That such a perspective has been generally neglected within what might broadly be termed orthodox Christian thought must of course be conceded. That such neglect has been a contributing cause for the sustained attack on the ancient christology of the Church will become apparent in the chapters which follow.

This brings to a conclusion our outline of classical christology. We can describe it as the publicly articulated set of beliefs about the person of Christ as true God and true man, conceived as the eternal Son of God incarnated as a human being for our salvation. It is the foundation of the distinctively Christian doctrines of God, human salvation, creation, anthropology and eschatology. Expressed formally in the Nicene Creed it has served as the unifying theological feature of the Church – Orthodox, Catholic and Protestant. It is, as we have argued above, a theological construction which has within itself sufficient resources to offer an able account of the person of Christ as he is made known in the Scriptures and experienced in the life of the Church.

In the sixteenth century the matrix of ideas that constituted this form of christology came to be challenged seriously. It was not just certain aspects of the classical architecture that were considered to be in need of refinement. The central pillars were themselves deemed to be fatally flawed. And it is the resulting breach with the ancient conversation, the willingness to clear the ground and start afresh in its theoretical construction of Jesus' person that characterizes modern christology. The second half of our study will examine the various reasons for the widespread disillusionment, particularly among Protestants, with the classical formulation and will test the adequacy of some of the structures that have been erected in its stead.

MODERN CHRISTOLOGY

CHAPTER SEVEN

THE SOCINIAN CHALLENGE TO NICEA

Modern christology can be described as the open and many faceted pattern of christological conversation, primarily within Western Protestantism that is marked by a clear breach with the classical model and the settlements achieved at Nicea and Chalcedon. It is a somewhat fragmented discussion informed and shaped by the philosophical and, in particular, epistemological concerns of modernity. In more recent times it has been characterized by a variety of imaginative but faltering attempts to rebuild, within the world of ideas which form its context, a successful christological theory. The rift between modern and classical christology can be traced back to Socinianism, a movement that came to birth in what has become known as the Radical Reformation and whose seminal ideas anticipate themes that were to shape much of Christian thought in the centuries that followed.

THE REFORMATION

Significant among the forces that gave rise to the Protestant Reformation in the sixteenth century was a widespread concern about eternal salvation and divine judgement. A dreadful uncertainty about the final outcome of one's own life and the lives of those one loved had long been a feature of medieval religious consciousness. The need for satisfaction to be made to God's honour or justice, the impotency of the human will, the role of repentance or penance in obtaining forgiveness and the possibility of preparing for grace had for a considerable time been matters of serious discussion in the Church. The novelty of the theology of the Magisterial Reformers, Luther, Zwingli and Calvin, lay in its radical critique of the Church's understanding of its own role in the administration of God's saving grace. The focus of the discussion was consequently not only upon soteriological issues such as faith, justification and grace, but also on the efficacy of the sacraments, the place of religious ceremonies, the ordering of the ministry and the authority of the Bible over tradition.

Apart from this ecclesiological critique, the Reformers, like their Catholic counterparts, lived in broad theological continuity with the ancient Church. They raised no questions over its classical christology or its doctrine of the Trinity. Lutheran use of the *communicatio idomatum* as a device to explain the presence of the physical body of Christ in the Lord's Supper was no more than the development of a strategy already employed by the Fathers for other ends. All the key building blocks of theological construction remained firmly in place. The debate between Protestants and Catholics over the meaning of justification was the outworking of a conversation that went back to Augustine in the fifth century. Vitriolic though it might often have been, it was a discussion within a shared conceptual framework and a common theological heritage.

There also emerged in the sixteenth century a conglomerate of religious groups which offered a far more radical critique of established theology than that of the Magisterial Reformers and which made no claim to share in the Church's ancient theological heritage. On the contrary, they were eager to challenge every aspect of that tradition. Significant among these were the anti-Trinitarians whose ideas were brought to prominence by Michael Servetus. He was a remarkable Spanish theologian, physician and humanist who, after relentlessly promulgating the view that Jesus was not the eternal Son of God, was burnt at the stake for heresy in Geneva in 1553. Fearing persecution from Catholics and Protestants alike, many other anti-Trinitarians sought refuge in religiously tolerant Poland, a sizeable body of them settling in the town of Racow. Their community prospered while there and its members became known as Socinians after Faustus Socinus, one of their most eminent theologians. Their theological school is reported to have had at one time upward of a thousand students, while their own printing press disseminated anti-Trinitarian ideas across Europe. They were eventually ejected from Racow in 1643 by the Catholics and some of their members came to settle in Holland and then England. Socinian views were to flourish spectacularly in this new intellectual climate. A large number of English

Presbyterian congregations came in due course to adopt them and formally embrace Unitarianism. But their effect on wider Protestant thought was more pervasive and influential than the size of the established Unitarian community might initially suggest.

THE *RACOVIAN CATECHISM*

First published in 1605 the *Racovian Catechism* was an articulate presentation of the body of Socinian theology with particular emphasis on the rebuttal of the orthodox doctrines of Christ's divinity and the distinct subsistence of the Holy Spirit. The style of the work suggests that its principal author, Faustus Socinus, was confident that an open-minded examination of the relevant biblical texts would undermine the orthodox position and persuade an unbiased reader of the truth of the Socinian cause. The Catechism patiently considers and answers almost every significant scripture that was being employed in the defence of an orthodox christology. It was published in a number of European languages and was used widely not only to instruct the Socinian faithful but to propagate their views in the broader community. Let us consider some of its principal themes.

Christ as Dependent on God

One of the key arguments of the Catechism is that Christ's empowerment by the Holy Spirit and his continued dependency on God, as it is reflected in his practice of private prayer are not compatible with the idea that he was substantially one with God:

> [T]he Scriptures explicitly declare that whatever of a divine nature Christ possessed, he has received as a gift from the Father; and refer it to the Holy Spirit, with which he had by the Father been anointed and filled . . . because Christ, repeatedly prayed to the Father: whence it is evident that he had not in himself a nature of that kind which would have made him the supreme God. For why should he have recourse to another person, and supplicate of him, what he might have obtained from himself? (*Racovian Catechism* 4.1, pp. 57, 59)[31]

To all who take the Gospel narratives seriously this is an argument of considerable weight. In the previous chapter we argued that

Chalcedonian christology does have within itself the resources to show why Jesus' human nature, being continuous with our own, is wholly dependent on divine grace and in particular on the empowering ministry of the Holy Spirit. It must be conceded, however, that those who have championed an orthodox view of Christ's divinity have generally failed to develop an adequate account of Jesus' dependence on the Spirit or of his need for prayer. And this failure has continued to provide an effective platform for those who would oppose the doctrine of the Trinity.

Christ as a Lesser Divinity

Using an argument similar to that of the Arians, the Catechism concedes that it is appropriate to ascribe to Jesus a measure of divinity, but not the status of the Supreme God:

> He was, however, not merely the only begotten Son of God, but also a GOD, on account of the divine power and authority which he displayed even while he was yet mortal: much more may he be so denominated now that he has received all power in heaven and earth, and that all things, God himself alone excepted, have been put under his feet. (4.1, p. 55)

Arianism had interpreted Christ as the incarnation of a pre-existing being who had been granted high divine honour but who was in himself no more than a creature. It failed, in part, because it was difficult to conceive, within a monotheistic world view, how this 'Word of God', who was brought into existence at the beginning of time and served as the instrument of all creation, could in himself be no more than a highly honoured creature. The Socinians avoided the difficulties raised by the postulation of a primordial created 'Word' by simply denying that Jesus was the incarnation of some pre-existent being. According to them, he had no existence prior to his conception in Mary's womb. He was not the agent of the creation of the world, neither did he sustain it. He was rather the agent of the new creation which came into being through the Gospel. Now the simplicity of this form of 'Adoptionism', the theory that Jesus was born as a mere human and adopted into a relation of divine sonship, offers an outwardly more coherent christological account than that of the Arians. Its exegetical problem, however, is with the strength of the biblical testimony both to the concept of incarnation and to Christ's pre-existent role as the agent through which the world came into being and by which it continues to be preserved. The Catechism's determination to give a reasoned answer to all of the appropriate Scriptures leads it to offer what appear to be more and more contrived explanations of apparently straightforward passages:

> But may not the old creation of heaven and earth be referred to Christ in some appropriate sense, which would indicate his high pre-eminence above the angels? Certainly; namely – in so far as Christ, being antecedently to all creation foreknown, especially chosen, and predestined to glory by God, was the cause of God's creating the world and all things, whereby he might carry into effect his purpose of conducting Christ to glory, and conferring through him eternal life on the human race: in which sense, in deed, the creation of heaven and earth and all things might justly be referred to Christ as its author; and this was of old known to the Hebrews, viz. that the world was created with a view to the Messiah. (4.1, p. 104)

Christ is the agent of the creation of the heavens and the earth because God formed them with Jesus in view. It is hardly a persuasive argument. The New Testament witness to Christ's role as the agent of divine creation at the beginning of time cannot be so easily sidestepped.

The Worship of Christ

It was a matter of some controversy among the Socinians whether or not Christ should himself be offered divine honour in their worship. In 1574, a dispute concerning the invocation of Christ arose between Francis David and Blandatra, the two leading theologians of the Unitarian churches in Transylvania. Following through the logic of Socinian discourse David had argued publicly that Christ could not with propriety be addressed in prayer since he was not God by nature. After an increasingly bitter debate, David's was eventually condemned by a council convened at Weissenburg. The Catechism gave firm support to the argument of Blandatra that it was appropriate to address Christ in prayer:

> But wherein consists the divine honour due to Christ? In adoration likewise and invocation. For we ought at all times to adore

Christ, and may in our necessities address our prayers to him as often as we please. . . . But if the angels, as they adore God, ought to adore Christ also, as a Lord given to them by God – how much more ought men to do this to whom he is with peculiar propriety given as a Lord, and to whom alone his is given for a Saviour! (5.1 pp. 189–190)

What is of particular interest is that the Socinians would not take refuge in the distinction made by the Catholics in explaining the difference between their veneration of the Virgin Mary and their worship of Christ:

They [the Catholics] deceive themselves by this distinction of terms [*latria* and *dulia*], since both these words signify service; and in every case wherein service is used for religious worship, it means *latria*, or such worship as is due to God alone. (5.1 p. 200)

The Socinians were not prepared to interpret their own worship of Christ as that which was due to any other but God. Nevertheless, they were careful to make a distinction between their worship of Christ and that which they believed was due only to the supreme God:

There is this difference, that we adore and worship God as the first cause of our salvation, but Christ as the second. We direct this honour to God, moreover, as to the ultimate object; but to Christ as the intermediate object. (5.1 p. 196)

By a strange irony the Socinian distinction here is remarkably similar to the way in which orthodox Christians have traditionally been called upon to worship the Father through the Son. We have suggested that it is the task of christology to give an adequate account of the person of Christ not only as he is made known in the Scriptures but also as he is encountered in the worship of the faithful. In short, the question must be asked of the Socinians whether they have provided an explanation of Christ's being which can properly account for the worship that they believe is his due. It is difficult not to feel some sympathy for Francis David whose argument that it was inappropriate to offer prayers and worship to a Christ who was not truly God appears to be far more logical than that of his fellow Socinians.

Scripture

To the question: 'But do you not acknowledge in Christ a divine as well as a human nature or substance?' the Catechism offers the following answer:

> If by the terms divine nature or substance I am to understand the very essence of God, I do not acknowledge such a divine nature in Christ; for this were repugnant to right reason and to Holy Scripture. (4.1, p. 55)

Suggested in this response is the Socinian methodological principle that theology ought to be determined by the examination of Scripture and the application of right reason. This hermeneutic strategy was to prove so influential in the development of theology that it might be of value to consider each of its aspects in a little more detail.

Our brief introduction to the *Racovian Catechism* will have indicated that the Socinians were clearly determined to derive their christology directly from the Scriptures. They embraced the post-Reformation watchword *sola scriptura* taking it to mean that no authority should be granted to the voice of tradition, including the creeds and other historical formulae of the Church. And having no authority they were deemed to have no value or place in theological construction other than as the false position of an adversary and so in need of rebuttal.

The appropriate methodology for theological formulation was held to be the unfettered examination of the Scriptures using the best critical tools available to determine the accuracy of the text.[32] Now the laudable idea that the text should be allowed to speak for itself can sometimes be a cover for a certain sleight of hand that is so deceptive that even its practitioners often fail to recognize it. Let me illustrate with a fictitious example. A Unitarian evangelist passes a copy of the *Racovian Catechism* to a seventeenth-century friend who worships in an English village church. She encourages him to read the book, and carefully look up all the relevant texts, so that his view of Christ might be shaped directly by the Scriptures and not by the liturgy, hymnology or recited creeds of his local worshipping community. He is attracted by the eminent reasonableness of the proposal and looks forward to studying a theology that is unencumbered by ancient church dogma and tradition and determined only by Scriptures. But the book that he has just been given as a guide is itself a well-developed interpretive theory of what the Bible actually means. It has been formed by 50 years of vigorous intellectual discussion within the Socinian community and refined through sharp debate with Protestant and Catholic theologians. The young Anglican's reading of the relevant scriptural passages at the book's recommendation will be mediated by what is in effect a carefully honed Socinian theology. There is, of course, always some form of mediation taking place whenever the Scriptures are studied in that there is always some interpretive framework, conscious or unconscious, that is being brought to the text and which plays a part in shaping our understanding. The mediation described in the story above is a 'closed' mediation in that it does not allow or suggest other mediating voices and disguises its own mediating function. And this is the congenital difficulty with any theology which purports to be wholly shaped by Scripture – it fails to acknowledge the mediating traditions that have determined its own construction and it often struggles to listen with any attentiveness to what other Christians might have discovered about the truth of the Bible. And these failures are, one could say, the besetting weaknesses of all sectarian theology.

Socinian theology is 'closed' in that it recognizes no need to interact seriously with an earlier christological conversation, however profound or enlightening it might have been. Such engagement is shunned not because the conversation partners are deemed unworthy or their conclusions trivial but because such discourse is simply not part of its theological methodology. An historic reason for this is that Socinian ideas developed and grew, not in the universities with easy access to the works of the Fathers, but among a lay community, in humble meeting-rooms and homes where the Bible and a growing assortment of Unitarian literature provided the bulk of the available reading material. Alienated from the ancient christological discussion both theologically and practically Socinians of the time encouraged their students to open their Bibles and form their views of Christ afresh, which in practice meant building on 50 years of Socinian interpretive insight. This practice is rather like encouraging a child to break up the largely completed family jigsaw puzzle and begin again so that this time he can do it by himself, properly, with just a little guidance. And this is one aspect of the methodological heritage that the Socinians bequeathed to modern christology – a propensity to discard all past christological achievement or dogma and to begin the whole project anew with scant regard to the work of others.

Reason

Socinians used the idea of 'reasonableness' as a tool in their criticism of orthodox christological ideas. It was a strategy which endeared them to many among the intellectual community of late seventeenth-century England. We need to remember that this was an age in which the application of mathematical reasoning by Isaac Newton had apparently unlocked the secrets of all movement in the universe, while John Locke had transformed epistemology with his carefully reasoned treatise on human understanding. Many now sought to demonstrate that religion itself was an eminently reasonable endeavour or that the sort of religion that was worthy of our support was able to acquit itself before the bar of reason. A number of influential books were written at that time on the reasonableness of Christianity.[33] Let us see then how the *Racovian Catechism* challenged the rationality of the orthodox view that Christ had both a divine and a human nature:

> Show me how the first mentioned opinion is repugnant to right reason? First, on this account, that two substances endued with opposite and discordant properties, such as are God and man, cannot be ascribed to one and the same individual, much less be predicated the one of the other. For you cannot call one and the same thing first fire, and then water, and afterwards say that the fire is water, and the water is fire. And such is the way in which it is usually affirmed; – first, that Christ is God, and afterwards the he is a man; and then that God is man, and that man is God. (*Racovian Catechism* 4.1, p. 56)

There are two elements to this critique of the two-nature theory of Christ's person. The second of them draws attention to the contradiction involved in ascribing human properties to the divine nature and divine properties to the human nature. In theology this practice of referring the properties of one nature of Christ to the other is termed the *communicatio idomatum*. It was originally no more than a linguistic tool. No claim was made that any actual transference of properties took place. Some theologians like Luther did, however, go further and used the idea to argue for a real transference of properties. Others such as Calvin held this to be wholly inappropriate. The Socinian contention that such a manoeuvre leads to a simple contradiction certainly carries weight. It is good to be reminded that the right use of reason requires us, even when we are discussing subjects that are mysterious or unfathomable, to avoid self-contradictory statements or plain nonsense.

The first part of the critique has to do with the unreasonableness of the orthodox proposal that one person is both truly God and truly human. This is a somewhat different issue from the one just considered. Christians have historically believed the incarnation to be a unique, foundational event. They have used it to reinterpret both their understanding of the manner of God's being and their assessment of what it is to be truly human. The person of Christ, as one who is both fully human and fully divine, is in this sense the Church's key hermeneutical principle. In a context where Christ is considered as the central interpretive reality, there is no weight to the argument that he does not satisfy some pre-existing criterion of what it means to be a person. The task of the Church is rather to submit to Christ as he is made known by the Spirit through the witness of the Scriptures and to bring its understanding about existence, the future, meaning and personhood into some sort of conformity to its mature reflection on the reality of Jesus.

Let me illustrate with another fictitious example. Sitting in a pub an artisan with no specialist scientific training is being introduced by a fellow drinker to some aspects of the Special Theory of Relativity. Between pints, he is told that all objects gain in weight and decrease in size when moving at great speed. He is incredulous. Our open-minded student from the university of life finds the ideas being bandied around the table fascinating but they make absolutely no sense to him within his current scientific frame of reference. Now we might ask: 'Is it reasonable for him to reject these ideas?' Certainly no blame can be attached to him for walking out of the pub totally unconvinced by the oversimplified account of the Special Theory or Relativity that he has just heard. But in due course if he is to go on and study applied mathematics or physics with any seriousness he will have to learn what it is to submit before a completely different scientific paradigm, and as he applies himself to his studies he will probably come to understand its inner logic and embrace its initially strange implications.

Although we tend to describe ideas that do not conform to our current world view as unreasonable they might in fact be perfectly logical. Christians believe that the Gospel of Jesus Christ sheds startling new light on the nature of reality. It offers a quite different paradigm of divine and human relations. Through it we gain fresh insight into ourselves, the character of God and the way he meets with us. Conversion to the Christian faith is consequently an entry into a new realm of thought, which operates with a quite different set of purposes, principles and values. It has its own inner logic. To those living outside this way of understanding, even its most basic assertions can appear strange and therefore unreasonable. The Socinian charge that orthodox Christian thought is 'repugnant to right reason' is sometimes no more than the assertion that its principles are those of a quite different world-view.

In its discussion of the nature of salvation the *Racovian Catechism* invariably interprets the relevant texts in a manner that affirms the place of human potency in the redemptive process. It uniformly supports what has historically been described as the Pelagian option, that is, the view that humans have within themselves the capability to contribute meaningfully to their own salvation. This optimistic assessment of human religious capability is linked logically to the Catechism's consistent opposition to the idea that Christ's death might have been in any way substitutionary or even necessary for our reconciliation with God. What is of significance for our discussion is that the idea of reasonableness is used to justify this particular soteriological perspective. Where the scriptural text opposes such an optimistic assessment of human potency, as it does repeatedly, it is put to the side on the grounds that it is 'repugnant to right reason' (5.8 p. 304).

We see then that within Socinianism the idea of 'reason' becomes linked with a specific theological agenda, positively described as the humanitarian reconstruction of the Christian faith. Negatively, one could say that in Socinianism reason serves as justification for resistance to a particular paradigm shift – to the changed perspective of the transformed Christian mind, the new awareness of human frailty and impotence and the discovery of divine grace and undeserved love. The anthropocentric humanism that the Socinian use of reason encourages is the second aspect of the legacy which it has left to modern theology. It is an emphasis which, along with the anti-credal tendency outlined above, was most clearly expressed in Liberal

Protestantism, a movement which was to deeply influence Western Christian thought till well into the twentieth century. The originality and potency of Socinian ideas are indicated in the fact that the definitive version of the *Racovian Catechism* was published in 1605, more than 200 years before the ways of thinking to which it gave rise came into full flower.

CONCLUSION

Until the advent of the Socinians, the view of Christ promulgated in the Nicene Creed of 381 continued without serious challenge for some 1,200 years. How effective was this new critique? Unlike the Arians, the original opponents of Nicene orthodoxy, the Socinians did not offer a clearly formulated alternative christology. What they did put forward was a loosely structured form of Adoptionism – Christ had no existence until his conception in Mary's womb and through the empowerment of the Holy Spirit he as a man received a form of divinity. How his person was unique, differing from any other person empowered by the Holy Spirit, was an issue that they did not address. Although Socinians offered Christ divine honour in their worship it is far from clear on what basis they were entitled to do this, for they explicitly denied that he had the nature of the Supreme God. In short, in their critique of the orthodox understanding of Christ they were unable to provide a coherent alternative christology to that of Nicea. They were, however, able to undermine the propositions of the Nicene Creed in the minds of many by the important questions they raised and through the methodology they introduced.

First, they asked why, if Christ was true God of true God, as Nicea indicates, should he still be dependent on the Holy Spirit and in need of personal prayer? It was a question that most contemporary theologians were ill-equipped to answer and led future generations of reflective Protestants to search for a more humanlike Jesus than that which the creeds appeared to offer. Second, Socinians developed a theory of interpretation which excluded the mediation of tradition in an understanding of the text, distancing themselves from the ancient christological discussion. Third, the Socinian emphasis on reason encouraged a somewhat mundane and human-centred religious approach that tended to discard from theology everything that did not conform to a pre-existing criteria of reasonableness.

Although the Nicene Creed continued to be recited in the Protestant churches of Western Europe at the end of the seventeenth century, a gap was beginning to open up between what these formulae actually signified and what many intellectually informed worshippers were coming to believe about Jesus.

Socinianism initiated a rift between modern and classical christology that was to expand over the next 300 years into what seemed to be an unbridgeable chasm. The questions Socinianism asked, the interpretative method it proposed and the rationality it encouraged came to their clearest expression in a theological school that sought to offer a historical account of the life of Jesus, the life-of-Jesus movement. An examination of the accounts of Jesus' life offered by two of its principal exponents will help us to understand why so many in the nineteenth century came to view Jesus as a quite different person from the Christ portrayed in the ancient creeds.

CHAPTER EIGHT

IN SEARCH OF THE HISTORICAL JESUS

The application of the methods of historical criticism to the Gospel accounts of the life of Jesus not only widened the gulf separating modern discussion about the person of Jesus from the classical formulations, but also called into question the very possibility of an intellectually credible christology.

In 1774, Gotthold Lessing began to publish as the *Wolfenbütteler Fragments* the polemical writings of Hermann Reimarus (1694–1768), a professor of Oriental Languages who had died 8 years earlier. Lessing's peers were divided over the wisdom of his action – some deemed it to be an act of great intellectual courage, others as one of supreme recklessness. Lessing was aware of the potential harm that Reimarus' writings could do to traditional Christian belief, but he trusted that their open publication might in due course lead to their refutation. Of particular significance among them was *The Aims of Jesus and his Disciples*, Reimarus' account of the life and goals of Jesus and the relation that these had to those of the early church.

REIMARUS' LIFE OF JESUS

The intention of Reimarus' historical reconstruction of Jesus' life was to discredit the Church's interpretation of his person and ministry. And it was his passion to achieve this goal that brought such clarity of focus and ruthless efficiency to his argument. Let us consider his analysis of the Gospel texts.

Reimarus held that the essence and purpose of Jesus' teaching were contained in the phrase: Repent for the Kingdom of Heaven has come near you. Jesus' proclamation of the Kingdom without any further explanation indicates that the concept was one already well-known to his hearers. It implied for them that the promised political rule of Israel by God's Messiah was imminent. Repentance was the appropriate way of preparing for this coming Kingdom for it was generally held among the Jews that it was 'the lack of repentance and moral improvement that would hold back the coming of the Messiah' (p. 38). And so along with the announcement of the approaching Kingdom of God, Jesus taught a deeper moral righteousness, requiring of the people a genuine conversion from their sins.

Although Jesus had a far deeper perception of the meaning of the law than the teachers of his day, he never sought to undermine or replace the Mosaic legislation as such. Neither did he, through the practice of baptism or in his final Passover meal with his disciples, intend to undermine either of these Jewish institutions. He introduced no doctrine of the Triune being of God or of his own substantial union with the Father. Being God's son meant no more to him than that he was particularly loved of God. Jesus, in short, did not seek to replace Jewish institutions, Jewish theology or Jewish law. It certainly was not his intention to found a new religion.

The Kingdom of God that Jesus proclaimed was one clothed in material splendour and was to be expected in the very near future. It would certainly occur during the lifetime of those who heard him preaching. Jesus astutely discouraged any who had recognized him as the Messiah from publicizing this insight before the appointed time. His intention was that the gathered worshippers would in their multitudes proclaim him as their king during the celebration of the Passover in Jerusalem. Entering the city on a donkey, in accordance with prophetic expectation, and clearing the Temple of those who misused it were highly seditious acts designed by Jesus to force the issue and so lead to his public acclamation as Messiah. But he misread the level of popular support that he had among the common people and was instead arrested by the authorities and executed as a Messianic pretender.

At Jesus' arrest, trial and execution his disciples betrayed great fear and lack of resolve. Their dreams of inheriting positions of power and material rewards in the coming Kingdom were dashed. A number of their leaders hatched a plan which would enable the Messianic movement to continue while they went on enjoying the comparatively secure and respected ministry which had maintained them for the past 2 or 3 years. They stole the body of Jesus before it putrefied and invited some of the other disciples to view the empty tomb. But, significantly, they made no public announcement of his resurrection for some 50 days, by which time they could claim he had already ascended into heaven and that further sightings of Jesus were not to be expected (p. 130). The apostles deftly transformed the message about the Kingdom of God coming in Jesus' lifetime to that of a Kingdom which would only be inaugurated when Jesus, having been raised from the dead, would return in great power and glory from heaven. The imminent expectation of the Kingdom remained, but in a radically altered form.

It is likely that as Jesus approached Jerusalem he had some apprehension that the whole undertaking might fail and shared with his disciples the possibility of his own suffering and death. In the aftermath of his execution it was these ideas that the apostles presented as being central to his mission. The essence of their new message was that Jesus, the Messiah, died for the sins of his people so that he might be for them as a spiritual saviour; that God raised him from the dead and that he would return in power to establish the Kingdom of God within the lifetime of the original hearers of the Gospel. This led to the formation of a religious system totally at odds with the Jewish religion which Jesus himself had practised. All the principal doctrinal elements of the Christian Church are consequently a complete distortion not only of the historical facts but also of the actual intention of Jesus.

As to his sources, Reimarus argued that the apostles naturally sought to retell the story of Jesus in a way that gave support to their new religious system and manipulated the history accordingly. Enough of Jesus' genuine sayings and deeds were, however, inadvertently left in the Gospel narratives for the possibility of a more accurate account of his life being constructed by careful historical and literary analysis. The reports of miracles are generally problematic and even if they can be substantiated they cannot by their nature establish the truth of any Christian dogma. Why should an inexplicable event ever prove the truth of a theological proposition? This also holds true for all alleged fulfilment of prophecies.

Reimarus' eighteenth-century account of the life and goals of Jesus in relation to those of the Christian Church is undoubtedly a potent piece of anti-Christian polemic. It offers a considered historical reconstruction of Jesus' life and its relation to the formation of the Church which, if true, undermines all the principal doctrines of the Christian faith. It puts forward no christological theory, for Jesus is held to be no more than a tragic Messianic pretender who was after his death grossly misrepresented by his own followers. Considering the subject matter of the sources the reader of Reimarus' work might be somewhat surprised that the relation of the divine and human with respect to Jesus' person is never considered. It soon becomes apparent that all such questions are excluded on methodological grounds. But if this is the case it is the methodology employed by Reimarus that is of particular interest to us and, as we shall see, determinative of later christological development in European Protestantism.

HISTORICAL METHOD

Although prominent theologians rose to defend the Christian faith in response to Reimarus' challenge, the project initiated by him was furthered by a number of able German Protestant scholars who continued till early on in the twentieth century to try and formulate a coherent historical account of the life of Jesus. They differed from Reimarus and from one another in their estimation of the reliability of the various sources, in their interpretation of the self-consciousness of Jesus and in their assessment of the purpose of his ministry. Nevertheless, in all of their studies Reimarus' basic methodological structure remained both intact and unchallenged. What were the determining features of his scheme?

In Chapter Seven we indicated how seventeenth-century Unitarianism had been shaped by two novel interpretive approaches. One was a total disregard of the theological discussions and doctrinal insights of earlier generations of Christians. There had been among the Socinians a determination to start theological construction afresh on the basis of the biblical text without any guidance from past christological development. The other approach entailed the use of the concept of rationality as an instrument of resistance to a shift of paradigm, a way of protecting one's world view from the strangeness of a scriptural perspective. Both of these tendencies were radicalized in the movement that sought to offer an historical account of Jesus' life.

First, in determining Jesus' history the movement discounted completely the theological interpretation of him given by his first-century Jewish followers. These Protestant scholars of the European

Enlightenment believed it was right to start afresh, not only with the assumption that all past christological formulations by the ancient Church were hopelessly compromised, but also that those whom Jesus had taught and commissioned to work alongside him had completely misunderstood who he really was or, at least, could not be trusted in what they wrote about his person. It was what we might now call a hermeneutic of deep suspicion. They began their investigation from a position of radical scepticism regarding the trustworthiness of the insights of everyone else. The unfinished christological jigsaw puzzle which had been meticulously pieced together through hundreds of years of Christian reflection and debate was now to be broken up, along with the perspective of Jesus' peers, so that the whole project might be started again without being distorted in any way by this ancient cloud of witnesses.

Second, the application of reason meant for the practitioners of historical-criticism conforming to the current canons of scientific enquiry. This included the ideal of the neutrality of the observer and an *a priori* predisposition against the supernatural or singular. That Reimarus and D. F. Strauss, two of the most formative scholars in the undertaking, were opposed to the Christian faith had no bearing on the significance of their work. Whereas an earlier epoch had assumed that one believed in order to understand, it was now taken for granted that if you believed you probably would not understand.[34] This was not a project in which people of faith sought in humble submission to understand the nature of the person whom they encountered in their worship and through the Scriptures. It was rather one in which any person with the appropriate skills in literature and history could through their creative skill and their technical management of the texts provide an account of Jesus which had the potential to overthrow all previous Christian interpretations of his significance.

One of the salient features of this methodology is that from the outset it precludes the possibility of a christological account of Jesus. It has within itself no mechanism to consider the relation of the divine and human in his person. All such references to such a relation in the Gospel sources were held to have no factual weight, they cannot: by its assumed canons of rationality, be considered as anything more than the subjective religious responses of his pre-scientific followers. There is consequently no narrated event, no word spoken, no prophecy fulfilled, no miracle observed, no outcome in the life of the believing community that could even in theory, according to this methodology, add the slightest weight in favour of a supra-mundane interpretation of the person of Jesus. It is of no surprise then, for all the brilliant scholarship of its practitioners, the life-of-Jesus movement could only offer an assortment of religiously mundane accounts of the man Jesus, accounts that could never adequately explain why a community who joyfully worshipped him alongside God the Father did in fact come into being.

THE ESCHATOLOGICAL JESUS OF ALBERT SCHWEITZER

Albert Schweitzer (1875–1965), who ably summarized this creative epoch and effectively brought it to a close, gives us a glimpse of the self-confidence, if not hubris, of the those who participated in this enterprise in the opening words of his classic work, *The Quest of the Historical Jesus*:

> When, at some future day, our period of civilisation shall lie, closed and completed, before the eyes of later generations, German theology will stand out as a great, a unique phenomenon in the mental and spiritual life of our time. For nowhere save in the German temperament can there be found in the same perfection the living complex of conditions and factors – of philosophic thought, critical acumen, historical insight, and religious feeling – without which no deep theology is possible. And the greatest achievement of German theology is the critical investigation of the life of Jesus. What it has accomplished here has laid down the conditions and determined the course of the religious thinking of the future. (p. 1)

He is partly right for this investigation has indeed posed questions which have shaped, directly and indirectly, the course of modern christology. The content and significance of these questions we will consider in due course. For now let us examine Schweitzer's own contribution to 'the quest for the historical Jesus'.

Schweitzer is an astute critic of the earlier lives of Jesus that had been offered by the dominant schools in German theology. He argues that for Rationalism 'the problem of the life of Jesus is solved the moment it succeeds in bringing Jesus near to its own time, in portraying Him as the great teacher of virtue, and showing that His teaching is identical with the intellectual truth which rationalism deifies'(p. 28). His analysis of Liberal constructions of Jesus is equally incisive:

> This want of insight into the largeness, the startling originality, the self-contradictoriness, and the terrible irony in the thought of Jesus, is not a peculiarity of Schenkel's; it is characteristic of all the liberal Lives of Jesus from Strauss's down to Oskar Holtzmann's. How could it be otherwise? They had to transpose a way of envisaging the world which belonged to a hero and a dreamer to the plane of thought of a rational bourgeois religion. (p. 208)

But in rejecting the perspectives of Rationalism and Liberalism we must not suppose that Schweitzer is offering a critique of the life-of-Jesus movement as such or is in any way seeking to undermine the project begun by Reimarus. On the contrary, he is one of its most ardent proponents. He accepts its basic assumptions and is faithful to its methodology. His disagreement with other interpretations of Jesus' self-consciousness and mission are differences of perspective with those who are, in effect, his fellow travellers on this journey of exploration. As with the other 'lives of Jesus' in this tradition, Schweitzer is able to treat Christ as a man who can be understood wholly within a world of natural causes and recognize in his death only failure and tragedy:

> The Baptist appears, and cries: 'Repent, for the Kingdom of Heaven is at hand.' Soon after that comes Jesus, and in the knowledge that He is the coming Son of Man lays hold of the wheel of the world to set it moving on that last revolution which is to bring all ordinary history to a close. It refuses to turn, and He throws Himself upon it. Then it does turn; and crushes Him. Instead of bringing in the eschatological conditions, He has destroyed them. (pp. 368–369)

Schweitzer differs with Reimarus' interpretation of Jesus' self-consciousness principally in that the Kingdom of God that Jesus proclaimed is held by Schweitzer to be eschatological rather than political in nature. According to him Jesus understood himself to be the heavenly 'Son of Man' referred to in Daniel, who would come in power and glory in the last days to establish a kingdom that was wholly discontinuous with the present world. It is an imaginative and insightful interpretation of Jesus' Messianic self-consciousness and it is instructive to see how Schweitzer develops it.

The problem posed by Matthew and Mark, the two oldest Gospels, is that the Messiahship of Jesus is portrayed by them as a secret that must be kept until his death. Jesus is himself conscious that he is the Messiah but he does not publicly put himself forward as such and very few of those around him are aware of his status. The popular solution in historical theology, that Jesus understood his Messiahship as a spiritual and moral reality while his disciples viewed it in political and material terms, has no foundation in the texts. Consequently, many historical critics have regarded the Messianic self-consciousness indicated in the Gospels as a later interpolation of the beliefs of the post-resurrection Church back into the life of Jesus. Schweitzer, however, maintains that an eschatological interpretation of Jesus' Messianic self-consciousness provides a way of treating these texts with greater integrity or historical seriousness.

He argues that only Jesus is fully aware that he is the heavenly Son of Man who will come in great power on the clouds to establish the Kingdom of God. It is in this sense that he knows himself to be the promised Messiah. When he sends out the twelve to proclaim the coming Kingdom, he warns them of the great trials they will encounter and promises that the Son of Man will come before they have gone through all the cities of Israel. But they return to him without having encountered the promised tribulation or witnessed the appearance of the Son of Man. They have, however, experienced in their ministry the power and authority of the coming Kingdom and rejoice accordingly.

From this moment Jesus' understanding of his ministry changes radically. He no longer believes that the disciples will have to endure great suffering in a time of tribulation which is the prelude to the coming of the Kingdom. It is he alone who will have to drink the required cup of suffering on their behalf:

> In the secret of His passion which Jesus reveals to the disciples at Caesarea Philippi the pre-Messianic tribulation is for others set aside, abolished, concentrated upon Himself alone, and that in the form that they are fulfilled in His own passion and death at Jerusalem. That was the new conviction that had dawned upon Him. He must suffer for others. . . . that the Kingdom might come. (pp. 386–387)

There is a possibility that two or three of his closest disciples who have declared their desire to share in the authority of the coming kingdom will also be required to share in the suffering. It is to these three that direct insight into Jesus' Messiahship is granted when he is transfigured in their presence, standing alongside Moses and Elijah.

According to Schweitzer the Messiahship of Jesus is initially known only to this small group until Peter, against Jesus' express instructions, declares it publicly to the other disciples at Ceasarea Philippi. Judas, now also aware of the secret, betrays the information to the chief priest. At the trial it is the charge of claiming to be the Messiah that is brought against Jesus. No witnesses are produced to testify to his guilt in this matter because there are none. Jesus is consequently required to testify against himself:

> The high priest said to him, 'I charge you under oath by the living God: Tell us if you are the Messiah, the Son of God.' 'Yes, it is as you say,' Jesus replied. 'But I say to all of you: In the future you will see the Son of Man sitting at the right hand of the Mighty One and coming on the clouds of heaven.' (Mt. 26.63b,64)

It is for blasphemy as an eschatological Messianic pretender that Jesus is executed. And so it is not surprising that he dies alone. If he had been a genuine political threat the Romans would not have been so unperturbed by his entry into Jerusalem. They would also certainly have taken action against his followers after his death. Jesus, however, never saw himself as a political Messiah, neither did the common populace. On the other hand, he is also not to be interpreted as a religious teacher of an earthly kingdom ethic for, according to Jesus, life in the new Kingdom will be a total dislocation from the life of this age – ordinary relations will be transformed. There will not even be marriage. Elements of his teaching which suggest that the coming of the Kingdom can be likened to the sprouting of a seed must not be interpreted to suggest that it will occur imperceptibly:

> What the parables emphasise is, therefore, so to speak, the in itself negative, inadequate, character of the initial fact, upon which, as by a miracle, there follows in the appointed time, through the power of God, some great thing. (p. 354)

Jesus, then, goes to his death alone. He now understands that he will pass through the tribulation on behalf of the elect. He alone will have to drink to the dregs the cup of suffering that is necessary to bring in the new age. The general resurrection, the advent of the Kingdom and the coming of the Son of Man in glory are a nexus of interrelated events that will occur simultaneously. Jesus dies, but the eschaton does not arrive. And ever since, the task of the Church has been to evade this, its greatest historical problem:

> The whole history of 'Christianity' down to the present day, that is to say, the real inner history of it, is based on the delay of the Parousia, the non-occurrence of the Parousia, the abandonment of eschatology, the progress and completion of the 'de-eschatologising' of religion which has been connected therewith. (p. 358)

The Jesus that Schweitzer presents is strange to the ears of modern religious sensibility. He is not a person who can easily be incorporated into its world view or theological agenda:

> In either case, He will not be a Jesus Christ to whom the religion of the present can ascribe, according to its long-cherished custom, its own thoughts and ideas, as it did with the Jesus of its own making. Nor will He be a figure which can be made by a popular historical treatment so sympathetic and universally intelligible to the multitude. The historical Jesus will be to our time a stranger and an enigma. (pp. 396–397)

Schweitzer's astute construction of the story of Jesus on the basis of the Gospels probably marks the point of greatest divergence between modern christology and the historic faith of the Church. It is ironic that this bleak assessment of the misguided mission of Jesus and his failed apocalyptic pretensions was put forward not by one of the opponents of the Church but by one who saw himself as its friend. Paradoxically, the spiritual barrenness of Schweitzer's conclusions is nowhere more apparent than in his attempt to sound a note of optimism in the face of them – an optimism which in the light of his own study can have no basis:

> Jesus means something to our world because a mighty spiritual force streams forth from Him and flows through our time also.

This fact can neither be shaken nor confirmed by any historical discovery. It is the solid foundation of Christianity. (p. 397)

What then are we to say of Schweitzer's outline of Jesus' history?

THE NATURE OF THE QUESTIONS POSED

There are a number of points that one might want to raise with regard to Schweitzer's account. On the chronology of Messianic disclosure, does not Mark indicate that Jesus openly referred to himself as the Son of Man from the beginning of his ministry and does not Peter's confession of the Messiah predate the transfiguration? Is Schweitzer being entirely fair to those elements in Jesus' teaching which imply that the Kingdom of God also has a personal or individual dimension as when a man finds a pearl of great price and sells all he has to posses it? Can the development of the Kingdom not also be understood as gradual and unnoticed like that of leaven in a loaf of bread? Is eschatological expectation as discontinuous with the present age as Schweitzer argues? If early Christians interpreted the day of Pentecost as a fulfilment of the apocalyptic prophecy of Joel then such language would seem to contain within itself a great deal of hyperbole. Nevertheless, criticisms such as these do little to reduce the offence that Schweitzer's account of Jesus brings to theology.

First, if the movement initiated by Reimarus is one which seeks to replace the Church's dogmatic interpretation of Jesus by a more liberal personage whose aims and methods are in basic harmony with the mindset of enlightened Western Europeans, Schweitzer dashes all of its aspirations. A person who believes himself to be the heavenly Son of Man, bearing in his body the suffering due to the elect in order to inaugurate the Kingdom of God, hardly accords with non-dogmatic Liberal sensibilities. It is no wonder that this whole undertaking all but came to an end with the publication of Schweitzer's work.

Second, a theology in which the issues of eschatology are located on the periphery of its religious concerns can hardly view itself as continuous with the teaching of Jesus or the expectation of the first community of Christians. A Christian theology that is true to its origins has to wrestle with the questions of the Parousia, the general resurrection of the dead and the final judgement. Any arguments for a realized eschatology must be held in some sort of dynamic tension with an account of all that has clearly not yet taken place. The problem of a delayed Parousia must be addressed with integrity.

Third, and significantly for our study, it raises important questions about the humanity of Christ. All of the lives of Jesus including that of Schweitzer offer a human history of Jesus. Can a Church which continues to confess the ancient creeds affirm that there is such a human history? More explicitly, does it allow that it is possible, at least in theory, to offer an historical account of Jesus' life based on his own Messianic self-consciousness without recourse to a supramundane interpretation of his psyche? In short, is a secular history of Jesus theologically possible?

The answer must surely be yes. If Doceticism, the view that Jesus only appeared to be a man is rightly to be rejected, then Jesus' words and actions impinged on human history and are open to historical investigation and assessment. His body was in principle the proper subject of any form of medical examination. If a lock of Jesus' hair was recovered from some ancient Palestinian garbage heap we could now, in theory, analyse his DNA. More significantly, if the Church was right to reject Apollinarianism, the view that the Logos replaced the human mind or soul in Jesus, then the working of Jesus' human mind was continuous with our own. His self-consciousness played a part in determining his decisions and actions. His culture, historical context and religion shaped the way he thought and acted. In summary, if the appropriate sources were available there is no theological reason why a coherent account of Jesus' human life should not be attempted using the tools of modern historical criticism.

CONCLUSION

We have here in this portrait of Jesus, introduced by Reimarus and brought to a measure of completion by Schweitzer, the essence of the problem facing modern christology. An interpretation of Jesus emerging from a historical critical study of the Gospels has been put forward which radically undermines not only the ancient dogma of the incarnate Son, but also every current conception of Christ as the proper object of worship, intercession or even imitation by the Church. The breach with classical christology, initiated by the Socinians some 300 years earlier, is now complete.

Confronted with this presentation of Jesus, the Western Protestant Church found itself faced with a twofold task if it was with integrity to proclaim Jesus as the object of its faith and the lord of its life within the world of ideas that constituted the European Enlightenment. First, it needed to learn how to speak about the things of God and, in particular, the divinity of Christ in ways that were persuasive within the age's prevailing theory of knowledge. Second, it had to come to terms with the historical–critical interpretation of Jesus, for this was a perspective that had been so firmly established by contemporary scholarship that it could neither be denied nor ignored. It is to the first of these projects that we now turn.

CHAPTER NINE

A THEOLOGY OF RELIGIOUS EXPERIENCE

How can humans know about God? As we saw in the previous chapter, the methodology employed by those who sought to offer a historical narrative of Jesus precluded any account of the divine either in Jesus' person or his ministry. This inability to address questions of divine agency or supernatural being was not merely a feature of an historical-critical approach to the Bible. It was a problem inherent in the theory of knowledge prevailing throughout what has become known as 'the Age of Reason'. Put simply, it was widely held that we could be certain only of those things that were in principle subject to observation and experiment. And the being and action of God clearly lay outside the scope of such scientific enquiry. Immanuel Kant, one of the most influential philosophers of the age, had proposed that beyond our empirical knowledge of the world we might postulate the existence of God, final judgement and heavenly glory to give some sort of account of human striving and moral accountability. But such knowledge always has a derived or conjectural status and lacks the certainty of the knowledge which is gained by direct experience. Traditional recourse to the authority of ancient testimony had been so discredited in the fields of cosmology and natural science that a direct appeal to the Scriptures or the Creeds for our knowledge of God, no longer carried weight among the literary classes. Further, any such appeal seemed to do no more than shift the present problem of how we might know God to an earlier age. How then was one to proclaim with credibility the truth of the Gospel and, in particular, the reality of Christ in such an intellectual climate?

FRIEDRICH SCHLEIERMACHER (1768–1834)

Schleiermacher had been brought up in the simple spirituality of Moravian piety but through his academic studies came to grasp the nature of the problem that modern thought posed for Christian faith and its talk about God. Eager to defend that faith, he sought ways of articulating Christian truth among those who inhabited the world of German modernity. His book *On Religion: Speeches to its Cultured Despisers*, along with his powerful public preaching, contributed to the influence that he came to wield on Protestant thought. Schleiermacher's imaginative strategy was to reconstruct theology out of the experience of human piety, that is, out of the religious self-consciousness. He argued that the essence of religion had to do not with knowledge or action, morality or aesthetics, but with a distinct feeling, a sense and taste for the infinite:

> The piety which forms the basis of all ecclesiastical communions is, considered purely in itself, neither a Knowing nor a Doing, but a modification of Feeling, or of immediate self-consciousness . . . the consciousness of being absolutely dependent, or, which is the same thing, of being in relation with God. (*The Christian Faith* p. 2,12)

With this imaginative manoeuvre Schleiermacher was able to side-step the epistemological problems associated with human knowledge of God. For, according to him, theology's concern is not with God as such but with human religious experience. This emphasis on human responsiveness to God as the primary subject matter of theology has its roots in early Lutheran thought. The Reformer, Philip Melanchthon (1497–1560) had famously argued that

> [i]f a man know nothing of the power of sin, of law, or of grace, I do not see how I can call him a Christian. It is there that Christ is truly known. The knowledge of Christ is to know his benefits, taste his salvation, and experience his grace; it is not, as the academic people say, to reflect on his nature and the modes of his incarnation.[35]

The monumental task that Schleiermacher embarked on was to transpose the whole body of Reformed dogma into a coherent systematic treatise generated only by an analysis of the human feeling of absolute dependence or God-consciousness. Each of the traditional doctrines and concepts were to be recast out of this material. For instance, sin was described in this way: '[W]e have the consciousness of sin whenever the God-consciousness . . . determines our self-consciousness as pain.' Similarly the work and the person of Christ find their relation to one another in the analysis of Christian consciousness:

> The peculiar activity and the exclusive dignity of the Redeemer imply each other, and are inseparably one in the self-consciousness of believers. (p. 374)

The outcome of this vast undertaking of Schleiermacher was the publication of his book, *The Christian Faith*, an outstanding work of the human intellect. In it the whole body of Lutheran dogmatics is reconstituted from a new perspective. There is a decisive shift from questions of metaphysics and the concern about ontology to an analysis of human subjectivity. Theology is no longer Christian reflection and talk about God as such, it has to do rather with the study of human piety:

> All attributes which we ascribe to God are to be taken as denoting not something special in God but only something special in the manner in which the feeling of absolute dependence is to be related to Him. (p. 194)

Schleiermacher was able to re-establish a place for theology in modern thought but at the cost of being able to speak directly of the things of God as they are in themselves, that is, apart from our experience of them. He could at best allude or point to the divine reality to which our own experiences and feelings are responses. In practice, however, Schleiermacher's talk about God often took remarkably objective form as he strayed over his own self-imposed boundaries and found himself engaging in traditional theological discourse about God. For example, at one point in his christological discussion he was able to make use of the highly sophisticated theological dogma that in God there is no distinction between resolve and activity (p. 401), a speculative insight into the simplicity of God's essence that appears to be far removed from an analysis of human religious experience.

Overall, Schleiermacher's new theological structure was somewhat different in shape from the Lutheran dogmatics on which it had been patterned. This is apparent in his treatment of the doctrine of the Trinity which instead of serving as the principal interpretative tool of theology, functions in Scheiermacher's work as a brief appendix and is considered by him to be not only highly problematic in its ortho-dox presentation, but lacking in any explanatory value. Although one might have expected Schleiermacher to have had difficulty with the objective nature of trinitarian dogma, it is somewhat surprising that there was no place in his system for the concept of divine mercy. He argues that: 'To attribute mercy to God is more appropriate to the language of preaching and poetry than to that of dogmatic theology' (p. 353). This conscious neglect of divine mercy or grace, something that Melanchthon viewed as a foundational element of all true Christian piety, must surely say more about the self-assured spiritual-ity of Schleiermacher's world than it does about the nature of the God to which the Scriptures bear witness.

SCHLEIERMACHER'S CHRISTOLOGY

How did Schleiermacher understand Jesus? Following his standard methodology he interprets him in terms of his God-consciousness:

> The Redeemer, then, is like all men in virtue of the identity of human nature, but distinguished from them all by the constant potency of His God-consciousness, which was a veritable exis-tence of God in Him. (p. 385)

Jesus is seen as being firmly embedded in the human community and condition. Like us all he has an absolute sense of dependence or God-consciousness. But, according to Schleiermacher, the perfection and potency of Jesus' consciousness means that there was in him a genuine existence of God. We have here a bold attempt to answer the key christological question: how can we say of Jesus that he was both truly God and truly man? Transposed into the language of human religious affections the question for Schleiermacher becomes one of the unity of our most unconditional adoration of him and our sense of brotherly comradeship with him (p. 391).

Schleiermacher's argument is that the 'ideality' of Jesus' human sense of absolute dependence or God-consciousness constituted a true existence of God in him. Many were to find in this apparently straightforward way of conceiving Jesus an intellectually persuasive christology. Let us consider its logic a little more closely.

What does Schleiermacher mean by the true existence of God in Jesus? He explains that it is 'the relation of the omnipresence of God to this one' (p. 387). The significance of this presence of God for Jesus' status or being, according to him, is that it serves as the ground for our unconditional adoration of him and for the communication of his perfection to us through the continuing life of the Church. Schleiermacher's unwillingness to use trinitarian conceptuality in his interpretation of Christ means that when referring to the presence of God in relation to Jesus he had no recourse to a doctrine of the Holy Spirit. Now, it is the testimony of the Church that the Spirit has been, from time to time, actively present among God's people, whether in prophetic inspiration, the empowerment of military leaders, the skills of the temple craftsmen or in the charismatic gifts and spiritual graces of the post-Pentecost Christian community. But, however great the manifest presence of the Holy Spirit in any of these people, there is never the slightest indication that they were afforded any degree of divine adoration or were at all worthy of such honour. That a particular intensity of human consciousness of God should be related to the presence of God, as Schleiermacher suggests, is right and proper. But such divine action or presence is properly referred to the person of the Spirit and it never implies that the recipients are themselves in any way divine. In short, that Jesus should have had an ideal God-consciousness can do no more than indicate that he is an ideal human. A theology such as Schleiermacher's, which fails to distinguish between the triune persons, does not appear to have within itself the resources to meet his own christological criteria. For if we are to interpret Jesus as one who is himself conscious of God through divine presence and is yet the divine ground of our own restored God-consciousness, we are in need of a trinitarian understanding of God. Using Schleiermacher's conceptual framework, we require a theology that is able to differentiate between God as the reality to which our own piety is a response, God as the imminent enabler of such piety and God as the one who in his human life among us reconstituted our broken piety by assuming us into his own perfect piety.

In attempting to present the Christian faith with intellectual integrity to the world of his day, Schleiermacher shifted our attention from the person of God to the nature of human spirituality, from theology to the study of religion. In doing so, he was able to introduce experimental and psychological ways of thought into Protestantism which allowed the key christological question to be posed and considered with intellectual credibility in the world of ideas generated by modernity. However, his interpretation of the divinity of Jesus in terms of the ideality of some form of human religious affection fails to explain why he should be the proper object of Christian adoration. Nevertheless, a path was opened by Schleiermacher along which those who had more robust proposals for our knowledge of Jesus' divine status were able to follow.

P. T. FORSYTH (1848–1921)

Forsyth was a Scottish Congregationalist who studied in Germany under the liberal theologian Albrecht Ritschl. He was later converted to Evangelicalism and came to the view that the cross of Christ was the key interpretative principle of theology and the basis for our knowledge of Jesus as divine. In his metaphysics, however, he remained indebted to the legacy of Schleiermacher, convinced that only the categories of thought generated from the world of human experience could speak persuasively to the modern mind:

> We work with such ethical categories – with ideas like personality, history, and society. These are what command thought, rather than ideas like being, substance, or nature, wherever thought works out its new creation in Kant and comes to close quarters with life. (p. 230)

Classical christology was deemed by him to have failed in its task, largely because of the limitations of its metaphysics of substance, being and nature, that is, its determination by an objective ontology:

> The truths [of the Chalcedonian Definition] were not really and inwardly adjusted, but only placed together; and they are thus the more easily shaken apart . . . and while the strongest assertions were made about the coexistence of the two natures as a postulate of faith, it was beyond the power of the metaphysic which then prevailed to show how they could cohere in a personal unity. (p. 217)

Forsyth believed that there was hope for the construction of a more effective christology using the new categories of thought brought into being by Schleiermacher, historical criticism and the field of psychology:

> But the metaphysic of history, the modern primacy of personality, and the new stress on experience, coupled with a critical historicism equally modern have opened a better way; and they keep Christ and his problem from retiring into the outskirts of thought. (pp. 217–218)

Nevertheless, Forsyth did not feel spiritually comfortable in the world of German Liberalism even though he had so unreservedly embraced its conceptual framework. He became deeply unsatisfied with what he saw as its humanistic self-assurance, its lack of regard for God's holiness, its failure to acknowledge human guilt and its inability to affirm unambiguously the true divinity of Christ. In due course he came to believe that it was through the proclamation of the cross that these perspectives could be most effectively challenged. Our particular interest is in Forsyth's attempt, in the context of the epistemological concerns of modernity, to use the cross to explain how it is that we might know Christ to be divine.

FORSYTH AND THE DIVINITY OF CHRIST

Forsyth held that the cross of Christ was the determinative idea for all Christian faith and theology. In particular, he argued that the person of Christ must be interpreted in the light of the significance of his death:

> It is the work of the cross that crowns and carries home the greatness of Christ. There the Master becomes our Lord and our God. Impression there becomes faith. And as faith can only have God for its object it is bound to pass, in the cultus at least, into the worship of Christ; and in theology it passes into the belief in his real deity, however expressed. It cannot be too often recalled that the article of Christ's deity is the theological expression of the evangelical experience of his salvation, apart from which it is little less than absurd, and no wonder it is incredible. (*The Person and Place of Jesus Christ* p. 74)

In this fertile passage lies the heart of Forsyth's argument for our knowledge of the deity of Christ. Whereas Schleiermacher had located the divinity of Christ in the nature of *Jesus'* piety, Forsyth sees it as lying in his role as the object of *our* piety. The Christian experience of salvation is the outcome of faith in Christ's redeeming work. Now, faith in Christ as redeemer cannot be distinguished from faith in Christ as divine or faith in God, for faith is a correlate of worship. Christ's deity is then, as he puts it, the theological expression of the evangelical experience of salvation. Within a theology of human subjectivity the recognition that Jesus is the object of our worship functions in a way similar to that of the 'homoousion' in classical christology. Jesus is divine as God the Father is divine. It is interesting that Schleiermacher was never willing to describe Jesus as the object of our unconditional dependence.

To strengthen his thesis Forsyth felt it was necessary to argue that Christ's redemptive ministry was not merely the agency through which God reconciled us to himself but that such a ministry was God's own immediate saving act:

The sinner's reconcilement with a holy God could only be effected by God. . . . The cross did not mean news that God was willing to receive us on terms which another than God should meet; nor that God sat at home, like the prodigal's father, waiting to be gracious when we came. But with God to will is to do; and the God who willed man's salvation must himself effect it – not accept it, and not contrive it, but effect it. . . . If a created being, however, much of a personal splendour, was the real agent either of revelation or redemption, then grace was procured from God, and not given – which is a contradiction in terms. For then the effectual thing was done not by God but by another. (pp. 85–86)

Forsyth has surely over-argued his case here. If every aspect of the redemptive work of Christ is a divine act, it is not clear why he needed to become human to win our salvation. The New Testament is, however, uncompromising in its insistence that reconciliation was also achieved through Christ as man. The letter to the Hebrews emphasizes that it is only one who is completely like us who is able to represent us as our high priest before God. Paul argues that as by human disobedience sin, death and condemnation came into the world, so through the obedient response of one man, the second

Adam, justification and life is won for the many. The mediator between humanity and God is reckoned to be the man Christ Jesus. Forsyth's theory that every aspect of Christ's redemptive work must be ascribed to his divinity is contrary to the consistent biblical testimony. It is a notion that can distort our view of the atonement and undermine the significance of Christ's human life among us.

However, Forsyth's insight that the experience of Christian redemption discloses the divinity of Christ does have much to commend it. Perhaps its most significant weakness lies in its failure to relate this revelatory event to the community of faith. The individual's experience of salvation does not occur in a vacuum, but is mediated through the presentation of the Christian story, the common narrative of God's saving action in the ongoing community of faith. The people of God who share in this common redemptive experience include the congregation of pious Jews who looked back to their rescue from Egypt and lived in holy expectation that God would act in fulfilment of prophetic promise to restore his Kingdom among them; the body of disciples who came to recognize through his teaching, miracles, death and resurrection that Jesus of Nazareth was indeed God's promised Messiah; the fellowship of early Christians that experienced salvation through repentance and faith in Jesus as it received the gift of God's Spirit and finally the family of the wider Church that has continued to honour the risen Jesus in its spiritual worship with a dignity equal to that which it bestows on the Father. It is through the communal redemptive experience of the whole family of faith, that the divinity of Christ is known.

Forsyth is significant for our study in that within the world of modern thought he offered an explanation for our knowledge of the deity of Christ in terms of human religious consciousness. Having found a way to speak about Christ's divinity it is interesting to examine what solution Forsyth brought to the central question of christology: How can we say of Jesus that he is both true man and true God?

FORSYTH'S CHRISTOLOGY

Forsyth had high hopes that the conceptual tools provided by modernity would enable the Church to construct a more effective christology than that put forward by the Fathers at Nicea and Chalcedon, limited as he believed they were by a metaphysics of being. He looked to the psychological concept of personality, rather than to the then popular Hegelian notion of the 'ideal', as a way to ground the unity of Christ's divine and human reality:

> But their reconciliation lies, not as Hegel said, with a superfined rationalism in a higher truth which is also of the reason, but in a supreme and absolute personality, in whom the antinomies work. (p. 71)

Forsyth's christology envisages the self-emptying or kenosis of a pre-existent divine person whose characteristics come to conform to the limitations of human existence. Alongside this divine self-emptying there is an equivalent movement or development of the characteristics of a human person towards divinity:

> Either the cross was the nadir of that self-limitation which flowed from the supramundane self-emptying of the Son, or it was the zenith of that moral exaltation which had been mounting throughout the long sacrifice of his earthly life, it was the consummation of the progressive union of his soul and God. I do not see why we may not combine the two movements. (p. 232)

> Christ thus embodies the two movements of spiritual reality in which man and God meet. (p. 339)

Forsyth describes this union of God and man as the mutual involution of these two personal movements in the one divine personality of Christ. The language and conceptuality are, of course, quite different from those which were employed in classical christology, but the shape of his thought can be quite easily mapped onto the framework of that earlier discussion. Against such a pattern, how are we to describe Forsyth's christological structure? His emphasis on the unity of divine and human within one divine personality gives his christological model a strongly Alexandrian flavour. But is it more than that? Without careful qualification, an Alexandrian christology, as we saw in Chapter Four, is always in danger of denying, consciously or unconsciously, a genuinely human mind or soul in Jesus and replacing it with that of the divine Logos. Does Forsyth avoid this drift into Apollinarianism? It is not clear that he does:

> A soul of Godhead is the necessary postulate of the redeeming personality; it is the necessary foundation of the growth of that

personality; and it is the necessary condition of the finality of his work. (p. 341)

To argue that there is in Christ a single divine personality with a soul of Godhead is bound to make it difficult if not impossible for Forsyth to interpret Jesus in his incarnate life as truly one of us, a man who thought, lived and acted before God as we do. It is instructive to see then how he understands the spiritual life of Jesus. According to Forsyth, Jesus' personal spirituality was quite different from our own:

> The religious problem for him and for us was not the same. He possessed the certainty and communion of the Father in himself. (p. 133)

Now if there was such an intrinsic spiritual certainty in Jesus it is hard to envisage how there could have been any doubt or temptation in his life; why he so struggled with the divine will at Gethsemane or why he had such a deep sense of separation from the Father on the cross. Most significantly such spiritual certainty would imply, as Forsyth recognizes, that Jesus was in no need of personal prayer: 'the Lord's prayer was given by him but not used by him' (p. 106). But an interpretation of Jesus as one for whom it is inappropriate to pray the Lord's Prayer is far removed from the portrait of him that is presented in the Gospel narratives.

Forsyth reaffirmed the divinity of Christ in a theological world which had lost confidence in its ability to defend it intellectually. He was unable, however, to go on and explain the person of Jesus in a way which affirmed how his human life and particularly his spirituality were continuous with our own.

CONCLUSION

The theory of knowledge which prevailed in the eighteenth and nineteenth centuries precluded any direct knowledge of God's being or action. It meant that apologists for the Christian faith had to envisage new ways of talking about God if they were to engage with the world of modernity with any intellectual credibility. With his wholesale reconstruction of Protestant theology in terms of human piety, Schleiermacher managed almost single-handedly to invent such a language about God and consequently stands out as one of the great intellects of his time. However, although he pioneered a way to speak with integrity to his age about the reality of God, his explanation of the deity of Christ fails to establish how Jesus is not merely the paradigm of Christian faithfulness but the proper object of Christian faith. Schleiermacher's theological construction did, however, provide categories of thought which allowed a later generation of theologians to affirm Christ's divinity in ways that were both continuous with the tradition and persuasive in the world of modernity. P. T. Forsyth was one of these; Karl Barth, whom we shall consider in due course, was another.

Forsyth argued that Christ's divinity was known from his role as the subject of the human experience of salvation. In a parallel project Barth was to argue that we know of Christ's deity from his agency in divine revelation. It would appear that after a long period of retreat and ineffectual defence the Church was at last finding the confidence, in the open marketplace of modern ideas, to talk about the divinity of Christ with a measure of intellectual assurance.

However, an inability to speak with credibility about the divinity of Christ was not the only intellectual difficulty facing the Church in the late nineteenth century. Her other challenge had to do with the portrait of Jesus that had been derived from the historical-critical study of the Synoptic Gospels. Such a view of Jesus appeared to preclude him from serving as the proper object of the Church's faith and worship. What response was the Church to give to this so-called Jesus of history?

CHAPTER TEN

THE CHRIST OF FAITH AND THE JESUS OF HISTORY

The 'Jesus of history' movement was motivated by the conviction that the standard portrait of Jesus presented by the Church had become so overlaid with the trappings of ecclesial dogma and Greek metaphysics that the underlying person had been completely obscured. Its self-imposed task was to peel off these strange ecclesiastical garments with which his devotees had so reverently adorned him and reveal to the world Jesus, the Jew from Nazareth, as he really was. In Chapter Eight we considered two of the more significant lives of Jesus. Using historical-criticism as their principal methodology and the Synoptic Gospels as their primary sources, such studies offered scholarly accounts of Jesus' life and self-consciousness which diverged sharply from the picture of Christ historically presented by the Church. They tended to portray Jesus as a man like other men, but in heroic mould, sometimes as a noble activist, ethical teacher or towering personality or, in Schweitzer's account, as a deluded prophet with fantastic apocalyptic expectations for himself. In none of the lives of Jesus, however, were there adequate grounds for this person to be considered as the proper object of Christian faith and worship.

How then was a worshipping church, open to the intellectual thought-forms of modernity and aware of the questions it posed to her interpretation of Jesus, to respond to the findings of the Jesus of history movement?

MARTIN KÄHLER (1835–1912)

Martin Kähler, the son of a Lutheran pastor was the professor of theology at the University of Halle. Although he was a prolific writer it was his short polemical work *The So-called Historical Jesus and the Historic Biblical Christ* that was particularly influential in enabling the Church to come to terms with the picture of Jesus put forward by historical-criticism. Kähler describes the general picture offered by the various lives of Jesus as the *'so-called* historical Jesus'. He argues that instead of revealing the truth of his person, the product of their study was a portrait that disguised Jesus as effectively as the dogma of classical christology:

> [T]he historical Jesus of modern authors conceals from us the living Christ. The Jesus of the 'Life-of-Jesus movement' is merely a modern example of human creativity, and not an iota better than the notorious dogmatic Christ of Byzantine Christology. (p. 43)

He offers a number of reasons why he believes the whole life-of-Jesus project is seriously flawed. First, the Gospel writers do not provide adequate or appropriate material for the construction of a history of Jesus. The purpose of their work was to create faith not to write history: 'Every detail of the apostolic recollection of Jesus can be shown to have been preserved for the sake of its religious significance' (p. 93). Somewhat paradoxically, Kähler uses the perceived unreliability of the Gospels as history to undermine the conclusions of the historical-critical studies and so defend the authenticity of the Church's traditional interpretation of Jesus:

> [W]e do not possess any sources for a 'Life of Jesus' which a historian can accept as reliable and adequate. . . . Furthermore, these sources cannot be traced with certainty to eyewitnesses. In addition to this, they tell us only about the shortest and last periods of his life. (pp. 48–49)

Second, there is no religious value in the history of Jesus as such. The potency of the apostolic message lies in the account of the redemptive work of Christ rather than in the details of Jesus' life. It was Kähler who first referred to Mark's Gospel as a passion narrative with an extended introduction. A description of the day-to-day events of Jesus' ministry is not of itself faith-inducing. 'If some people have in fact acquired their faith in the Saviour from the

Gospel accounts . . . then that would only show that exceptions prove the rule' (p. 83). Kähler believes there is only a limited value for Christian faith in the biographical details of Jesus' life:

Do I really need to know more of him that what Paul 'delivered to [the Corinthians] as of first importance . . . that Christ died for our sins in accordance with the Scriptures, that he was buried, that he was raised on the third day . . . and that he appeared'. (p. 60)

Third, the methodology employed by the life-of-Jesus movement is unsound. It 'must, in view of the silence of the sources, use as a means of research the principle of analogy with other human events – thus contradicting the whole tenor of the Gospels portrayal of Jesus' (p. 52). Jesus, as sinless, is unique which means that the principle of analogy on which historical reconstruction is so reliant cannot be an appropriate way to envisage the contents of his self-consciousness. But it is precisely the imaginative reconstruction of his inner thoughts and religious motivation which lies at the heart of the various 'lives of Jesus'. Those who would write a coherent history of Jesus have to have recourse to an outside force to rework the fragments of the tradition. And 'this force is nothing other than the theologian's imagination – an imagination that has been shaped and nourished by the analogy of his own life and of human life in general' (p. 55).

Fourth, Christian faith cannot be made to wait on the results of scientific study. 'For historical facts which first have to be established by science cannot as such become experiences of faith' (p. 74). If faith was dependent on academic proficiency only informed scholars would be authentic Christians.

Positively, Kähler offers an alternate picture of Jesus, the historic biblical Christ, as a more faithful image of his person. This portrait is described as historic (*geschichtliche*) in that it exercises a discernible personal influence upon later generations (p. 63). Kähler here makes use of the view, widely held in liberal Protestantism, that Jesus continues to influence modern piety and sensibility through his extraordinary historic personality. He argues that the decisive influence that Jesus has upon posterity can consist only in the faith of his followers. What is it that induces this faith? It is the theological or dogmatic picture of Christ drawn from the whole Bible and made known in the proclamation of the Church. This picture of the biblical Christ is an image which was initially pressed onto the minds of his disciples by Jesus himself:

[I]n his unique and powerful personality and by his incomparable deeds and life (including his resurrection appearances) this Man has engraved his image on the mind and memory of his followers with such sharp and deeply etched features that it could be neither obliterated nor distorted. (pp. 89–90)

In the preaching of the Gospel it is this picture, not of an extraordinary human being, but of Christ preached from and in faith, that challenges the hearer. 'In making a decision when confronted by this picture . . . two impelling forces interact. The one is receptivity . . . the other force is the impression which this marvellous picture makes upon the receptive beholder' (p. 78). In short, the picture of the biblical Christ, communicated in the proclamation of the Gospel is effective in producing faith and so 'historic'. The picture of the historical Jesus is not.

The doctrine of justification by faith is the formative principle of all Kähler's theology. Faith consequently becomes for him the subjective criterion by which the adequacy of all theological thought can be adjudged. So it is that Kähler understands Jesus' theological significance as being determined by the influence he has for Christian faith. Further, he argues that the authenticity of the picture of Jesus can be assessed by the response that believers make to it: 'The passionately held dogma about the Saviour vouches for the reliability of the picture transmitted to us by the biblical proclamation of Jesus as the Christ' (p. 95). Kähler seeks to avoid what appears to be the hopeless circularity of this argument by insisting that it is Christ who initially impressed this image on the minds of his followers through the power of his personality and the events of his life. There is then behind the 'picture' of the biblical Christ an objective person. However, the controlling metaphysics of a subjective faith do not seem to allow anything further to be said about him. We have immediate access only to the 'word-picture' of Christ presented to us in Christian proclamation.

Was Kähler successful in undermining the portrait of the historical Jesus presented by the life-of-Jesus movement? It is not an easy question to answer. Within a few years the whole process which came to be described as the original quest for the historical Jesus was brought to a close with Schweitzer's contribution, outlined in the previous chapter. A number of significant German theologians, including Rudolph Bultmann, Karl Barth, Emil Brunner and Paul Tillich went on to develop in their own directions many of the ideas that had been put forward by Kähler. In the light of their work Liberal Protestantism, which had spawned the Life-of-Jesus movement, was widely considered to have been exposed as a bourgeois, anthropocentric expression of the Christian faith. Nevertheless, as we shall see in Chapter Twelve, questions about the history of Jesus were to return again, demanding to be taken more seriously. Negatively, Kähler's polemic against the 'Jesus of history' encouraged a polarization between theological and historical accounts of Jesus which continues to be reflected in some measure in the ongoing disjunction between the disciplines of theology and biblical studies. It is surely an unsatisfactory situation. The roots of such polarization are christological and it is to the christological implications of Kähler's thesis that we now turn.

KÄHLER'S CHRISTOLOGY

Kähler along with many in his theological world was deeply dissatisfied with the metaphysics of classical christology and the 'picture' of Jesus that it presented. He was, however, in support of its principal objective:

> [T]he purpose of all dogmatics is, or ought to be, merely to guard a simple catechetical statement, namely that Jesus Christ is true God and true Man, against all kinds of attacks and obscurations, past and present. (p. 102)

With this goal in mind he offers a thoughtful account of the divinity of Christ in terms of the subjective language of human faith:

> For the divinity of Christ, however it may be more precisely defined in theology, means for us: that by virtue of which he may become the object of faith, without this faith's coming into conflict with the First Commandment and without it leading to deification of the creature. (p. 104)

Such a description of Christ's divinity is similar in its structure to that of Forsyth, outlined in the previous chapter, although it places greater weight on the objective pole in the knowing relationship. Christ's deity is not simply the theological expression of the evangelical experience of salvation; it is that reality about Christ which makes him the proper object of justifying faith.

What has Kähler to say about the humanity of the biblical Christ? This is a little more problematic for him and there is less clarity in his exposition. He looks to the Gospels for a portrayal of Christ's human life:

> One might say . . . that the Christ of the Gospels is 'the transparency of the Logos,' with the qualification that this diaphanous medium is not a nebulous legend but a tangible human life, portrayed in a rich and concrete though brief and concise manner. (p. 95)

The physical human life of Jesus is the medium through which the Logos is known. It is not a heavy veiling of his divinity but a 'transparency' through which his deity is manifest. But is Kähler then implying that the 'Jesus of history' is a trustworthy portrait of Christ's humanity? There are indications that he is. For he can on occasion speak of the historical Jesus, not as a false and distorting portrait of Jesus, but as the description of a person whose history is open to our examination:

> It is clear that the historical Jesus, as we see him in his earthly ministry, did not win from his disciples a faith with power to witness to him, but only a very shaky loyalty susceptible to panic and betrayal. (p. 65)

This is a revealing and highly significant comment. It suggests that the historical Jesus is on occasion viewed by Kähler not as a false portrait constructed out of the Gospels by a faulty methodology but as an accurate account of a person who prior to the events of Easter was spiritually ineffective. This identification of the humanity of Christ with the historical Jesus might be the result of some categorical confusion on Kähler's part but it was to prove formative in the ongoing christological discussion. The historical Jesus came to mean in much twentieth-century theology simply Christ as man.

Conversely, although it undermines the coherence of his original argument, Kähler could sometimes speak of the biblical Christ as though he was referring directly to the Logos or the divine Son:

The biblical Christ is the great vital power who has reinforced the message of the church from within. (p. 104)

And so, counter to the logic of Kähler's initial thesis, the relation between the Christ of faith and the historical Jesus came to suggest, particularly in German theology, the relation between the Word of God and the humanity of Christ, the divine and the human in Jesus. Throughout this book we have suggested that it is the principal task of Christology to delineate and explain the nature of this relation. Let us see then how two of the major figures of twentieth-century theology, Rudolph Bultmann and Karl Barth, were to deal with it.

RUDOLPH BULTMANN (1884–1976)

Bultmann is unusual among modern academic theologians in that he is also a highly respected New Testament scholar. In his writing a number of the arguments put forward by Kähler in response to the portrait of the 'Jesus of history' are developed and incorporated into his own imaginative theological system.

As was the case with Kähler, Bultmann's theology is determined by his understanding of faith. Faith is, for him, a form of obedience rather than knowledge; a personal deed of decision rather than a pious experience; the acceptance of a word of God rather than a general trust in his faithfulness. Its object is always God's saving act in Christ. In existential terms, it is the individual's present and repeated decision for authentic existence, an action in which the believer is personally engaged by the word of God.

Kähler's argument that the Gospel writers' motivation was to create faith rather than to write a history, was developed by Bultmann in the application of Form Criticism to the Gospel narratives. The structure or forms of self-contained sections of these books were analysed according to their religious motivation or function. The question was asked: what do we learn of the Church from the fact that it preserved this particular piece of writing in this precise form? Bultmann used the insights acquired from such analysis to trace the religious development of the earliest Christian community and so explain how the one who proclaimed the Gospel became, after the events of Easter, the content of the Church's proclamation. He also offered an account of how the Church came by stages to attribute divine status to Jesus:

> The titles the Church conferred upon Jesus to indicate his significance and dignity were borrowed from the tradition of Jewish messianic faith, in which motifs of diverse origin were admittedly united. . . . In any case, the earliest Church did not cultically worship Jesus, even if it should have called him Lord; the Kyrios-cult originated on Hellenistic soil. (*Theology of the New Testament* vol. 1, pp. 48–49,51)

Recognizing how various 'objectifying' features had been introduced to the narrative by the Church, Bultmann sought to 'deconstruct' the Gospel story in order to uncover its essential message. He described this process of getting behind the external forms of the narrative in order to expose the heart of the Gospel as one of demythologization.

Bultmann shared with Kähler the view that the details of the Gospel accounts including the sayings of Jesus are insignificant for faith. 'The message of Jesus is a presupposition for the theology of the New Testament rather than a part of that theology itself' (*Theology of the New Testament*, vol. 1, p. 3). He believed that the Danish philosopher, Soren Kierkegaard, was essentially correct in his assertion that the tradition about Jesus is adequately presented if one says that 'we have believed that in such and such a year God showed himself in the lowly form of a servant, lived among us, and taught, and then died.'[36] The pivotal question for the Jesus of history movement: 'How did Jesus understand his own mission?' is, according to Bultmann, of no consequence for faith:

> [I]f the fact should be established that Jesus was conscious of being the Messiah, or the Son of Man, that would only establish a historical fact, not prove an article of faith. Rather, the acknowledgment of Jesus as the one in whom God's word decisively encounters man, whatever title be given him – 'Messiah (Christ),' 'Son of Man,' 'Lord' – is a pure act of faith independent of the answer to the historical question whether or not Jesus considered himself the Messiah. Only the historian can answer this question – as far as it can be answered at all – and faith, being personal decision, cannot be dependent upon a historian's labour. (p. 26)

Christ as the object of Christian faith and worship becomes for him totally insulated from any possible outcome of historical research. It does not actually matter what Jesus thought of his own status, his calling and his mission. These are questions for the historian not the theologian. His virgin birth, his resurrection, his ascension and his eschatological return in glory do of course provide the form that the proclamation of the Gospel takes historically. But we must demythologize this narrative if we are to discover the essence of the message that it holds and present it afresh to this generation. What is this essence? Jesus is the one in whom God's word decisively encounters men and women. This is known only in faith and faith is independent of historical study.

The historical Jesus is then for Bultmann not a false portrait of his person constructed from a faulty methodology. He is, rather, a concrete human being, a person of history open to scholarly, historical-critical examination. From his own analysis of the Gospels Bultmann is confident that: 'He does not proclaim himself as the Messiah, i.e. the king of the time of salvation, but he points ahead to the Son of Man as another than himself' (p. 9). Overall Bultmann's account of the historical Jesus is as theologically sceptical as any of those offered by the life-of-Jesus movement. The purpose of his scepticism, however, is not like that of Reimarus, to undermine the faith of the Church, but rather to encourage it or, more precisely, to make room for its possibility. Bultmann believes that faith has to be rescued from the human inclination to objectify God's actions if it is to truly encounter the inexpressible mystery of his saving event in Christ. This temptation to objectify or in some way externalize the Gospel into a dogmatic formula or religious text is for him the antithesis of authentic faith:

> But does that [seeking authority in the objective text] not shift the real basis for the power of the gospel message and for the Christian's own security by putting a faith in the letter in place of the genuine faith which seizes the word of God's grace addressed to one's conscience and self-understanding – seizes it on the basis of having been inwardly conquered by it and not on the basis of rational proofs? (p. 117)

If Bultmann's outline of the historical Jesus gives an account of who Jesus actually was, how can this remarkably ordinary person serve as the object of Christian faith? Bultmann's answer is that it is not the historical Jesus but the Christ of Christian proclamation, the kerygmatic Christ, who is the proper object of faith. The kerygmatic Christ is a portrait of Jesus. It offers what Bultmann describes as a storied-account of his person. It is the theological interpretation of him in terms of the Old Testament messianic images and the forms of the religious cultus. The New Testament theologians, especially Paul and John, gave important shape to this theological interpretation of Jesus, going well beyond the historical Jesus' own self-understanding. Their contribution is, consequently, as essential to the picture of the kerygmatic Christ and so to God's saving purposes as the life of the historical Jesus. Bultmann believes that one can find in Paul and John a determination to demythologize the traditions which they had received so that they might present the bare essence of the Gospel as encounter with God through faith in his saving action in Christ.

The kerygmatic Christ is then the theological portrayal of the historical Jesus as it occurs in Christian preaching. The historical Jesus is dead. He is not personally present in the proclamation, but the fact of his life and death, what Bultmann calls the historical *Dass*, is the reality that undergirds it. The vital link between the kerygmatic Christ and the person of the historical Jesus lies in the essence of Jesus' message. The historical Jesus called his hearers to an eschatological decision of faith. And this is also the heart of Christian preaching.

The believer meets not the historical Jesus in the proclamation of the Gospel but the Risen Lord. 'Christ the crucified and Risen One, encounters us in the word of proclamation – nowhere else' (*New Testament and Mythology*, p. 40). By the 'Risen Lord' Bultmann does not mean the historical Jesus resurrected from the grave. For him the objective bodily resurrection of Jesus has no particular significance for theology. The 'Risen Lord' is not a reality to be objectified in such a way. He speaks of it rather as God's eschatological event of salvation in Christ. In the existential act of faith the believer encounters the resurrection or life-giving power of Jesus Christ, through the preaching of the Church. Jesus Christ as the *Christus Praesens* is the one encountered through the proclamation of the Gospel and as such he is both the object and the author of faith.

What are the christological implications of all this? In the historical Jesus Bultmann recognizes a fully human life. In the eschatological act of divine salvation he holds that the believer encounters the risen

Lord. Both of these realities, the human life and the divine saving action, are identified by him with the person of Jesus Christ. Many commentators, including his colleague Karl Barth, confess their inability to understand how Bultmann is able to relate the historical life, the kerygmatic portrait and the eschatological event to the one person of Jesus Christ. Although Bultmann does not offer a conceptually clear explanation of these relations, he does indicate that we find a connection between them in the preaching of the historical Jesus. 'Jesus' call to decision implies a christology' (p. 43). This does not resolve all the logical difficulties that Bultmann's exposition raises, but perhaps we should not expect it to do so. Bultmann practises his theology within a subjectivist paradigm, as suggested in his comment: 'It is clear that if a man will speak of God, he must evidently speak of himself.'[37] For Bultmann, Christians are confronted with various christological phenomena: an historic account of the man Jesus that can be scientifically established from the Gospels; a theological interpretation of Jesus presented in the Scriptures and Church proclamation; Christ as subject of the divine saving event in the act of faith. To try and offer an objectifying and intellectually satisfying account of the relation between these phenomena would, he believed, undermine the existential act of faith as radical trust in the saving act of God. Nevertheless, his assertion that Jesus is both a fully human life and a divine saving event provided the conceptual framework within which the christological question came to be addressed in the twentieth century. Let us take a moment to clarify this.

DIVINE AND HUMAN REALITY

Stated loosely, the central task of christology, as it has been understood historically, is to explain the relationship between the divine and human realities that constitute the person of Jesus Christ. But such an exercise presupposes that the prior question about the *loci* of those realities has already been settled successfully. For example, in a classical incarnational christology the human reality was considered to be to an *enhypostatos physis*, that is, one whose existence can never be considered apart from its union with the eternal Son of God. The divine reality was held to be the eternal Son of God. In their hypostatic union they constituted the *hypostasis* or person of Jesus Christ, the one who is both truly God and truly man. For Bultmann the locus of Jesus Christ's human reality is the historical Jesus, the human person who lived and died in Palestine and whose history is open to the normal methods of scientific enquiry. The primary locus of the divine reality is what he terms the Risen Lord or the word of God, identified by him as the divine eschatological and saving event encountered existentially by the believer in the act of faith. The unqualified identification of the divinity of Jesus Christ with this saving event is the key conceptual shift which differentiates early twentieth-century christology from that of the ancient church. In traditional dogma the divine saving and revealing act to which Bultmann refers was considered to be an immediate act not of Jesus Christ but of the Holy Spirit.

CONCLUSION

The life-of-Jesus movement sought to strip the theological robes from the person of Jesus and present him as no more than an exceptional man of history, cast from the same physical and psychological material as the rest of us and constrained by the religious, intellectual and social limitations of his community and time. But a person such as this could clearly not be the proper object of the Church's unconditional trust and worship.

Kähler argued that the 'historical Jesus' was in fact a false portrait, disguising rather than revealing his true person. He offered an alternative and spiritually more effective picture; one derived from the apostolic testimony and the witness of Scripture and made known in the preaching of the Church; one which he described as the historic biblical Christ. In due course, however, the distinction between the historical Jesus and the Christ of faith came in theology to suggest not two alternative portraits of him but two quite different ontological realities, human and divine, both of which referred to this one person.

Bultmann developed Kähler's thesis in significant ways. He understood the historical Jesus to be a proper subject for historical research, although his person and mission were held to be of limited significance for faith. The kerygmatic Christ is, in contrast, a theological or storied account of Jesus and the focus of Christian belief. Although this portrait of Jesus has been objectified by the earliest church with mythological interpretation, it contains the essence of the Gospel promise and through its proclamation the believer encounters the eschatological saving act of God in Christ, that is, the risen Lord or word of God.

Bultmann's christological presentation is imaginative, complex and not always easy to follow, leaving itself open to misunderstanding and caricature. His ideas are those of a gifted biblical scholar and deeply reflective theologian who has had a significant influence on twentieth century Christian thought and whose work is worthy of serious consideration. Bultmann's lack of clear dogmatic structure in his christological presentation is partly due to his fundamental opposition to an objectifying account of Christ. This aversion to any form of objectivism is a product both of his existential understanding of faith and his commitment to the subjectivist paradigm that had dominated theology since Schleiermacher. It meant that he made no systematic attempt to clarify the relations between the various christological phenomena encountering the Christian, that is, the historical Jesus, the kerygmatic Christ and the eschatological saving act related to the act of faith.

In his theology Karl Barth laid great emphasis on the transcendence of God and within the objectivist framework that such an emphasis generated was able to offer an explanation of the nature of these relations. It is to his exposition of them that we now turn.

CHAPTER ELEVEN

THE DOCTRINE OF THE WORD OF GOD

KARL BARTH (1886–1968)

One of the reasons for the abiding popularity of Karl Barth's theology is its ability to transport its readers from the spiritual barrenness of both the historicism and subjectivism which had dominated nineteenth-century religious thought to a place where God is spoken of with fluency and delight.[38] Alongside his confident objectivism, it is the introduction he provides, through the Reformers and the Church Fathers, to the theological discussion of the historic church that makes the reading of Barth so interesting for those who have given time to it. As a brilliant conversationalist he engages imaginatively and creatively with the great dogmatic themes that have been the subject of Christian reflection from the earliest times.

John Webster, in his book *Karl Barth*, made the following, illuminating comments on Barth's motivation:

> [H]is work was permanently stamped by the experience of feeling the need to reinvent the discipline of Christian theology. (p. 30)

> At other times, Barth's procedure is not to attempt a conceptual translation of the language of faith, but simply to offer a reflective expansion of a biblical or credal phrase – precisely because dogmatics is not an enhancement of faith's primary ways of speaking abut God, but merely a discursive repetition whose aim is nothing more than saying what has already been said. (p. 62)

Barth can be properly viewed as both a theological innovator and as one who sought to lead theology back to the dogmatic tradition of the historic Church, to heal the breach that had been created between modern and classical christology. His extensive reading of the Reformers and the Church Fathers meant that that the concepts and ideas developed in these traditions were not only increasingly incorporated into his own system but served to give shape and direction to his whole project. Consequently, many of his christological ideas, such as the one below, came to mirror the classical formulations of Nicea and Chalcedon even though, as we shall see, they do not flow naturally from his doctrine of the Word of God:

> From the second statement, that the existence of the Son of God became and is also that of a man, the man Jesus of Nazareth, there follows the third, that in the one Jesus Christ divine and human essence were and are united. This statement brings us to the doctrine of the two natures in the strict sense. It says something that cannot be relinquished and therefore cannot be evaded. (*CD* vol. I.1, p. 60)

Our focus in this chapter is not on those aspects of Barth's work that reflect his commitment to reaffirm the tradition, to say again what has already been said. It is, rather, to use Webster's phrase, on the set of ideas around which he sought to 'reinvent the discipline of Christian theology' – his concept of revelation and the related doctrine of the Word of God.

REVELATION

Barth brought about a change in the focus of Western theology as significant as that effected by Friedrich Schleiermacher a 100 years earlier. Believing theology's primary task to be an examination of the Church's talk about God rather than an analysis of human religious experience, he sought to shift theological attention from the human subject of faith to its divine object and proper ground. Barth's new perspective was the outcome of a conscious break that he had made with the theological liberalism of his teachers, disillusioned by their collusion with the ideology of the First World War and convinced, particularly from his study of the Epistle to the Romans, of the need to emphasize anew the transcendence, freedom and absolute otherness of God.

Although Barth renounced the direction that was being taken by the theological scholarship of his age, his own work continued to be

shaped by the epistemological concerns of modernity and its sceptical attitude towards the possibility of human knowledge of God. His
response, however, took a quite different form from that of his teachers. He argued that we can speak about God not as a derivative of
our study of human spirituality but because God reveals himself to
us. To the question: 'Who is this God who makes himself known?' he
answered that it is the one who exists in three modes of being as
Revealer, Revelation and Revealedness:

> *God* reveals Himself. He reveals Himself *through Himself*. He
> reveals *Himself*. If we really want to understand revelation in
> terms of its subject, i.e., God, then the first thing we have to realise
> is that this subject, God, the Revealer, is identical with His act in
> revelation and also identical with its effect. (*CD* vol. I.1, p. 296)

Although revelation is a divine act, Barth acknowledges that it must
always be recognized as God's speech to humans. 'Hence we cannot
speak or think of [revelation] at all without remembering at once the
man who hears and knows it' (*CD* I/1, p. 191). Revelation is an action
that takes place in the human religious consciousness. But this human
locus of the revelatory act creates a serious problem for his understanding of God. Barth rightly affirms that: 'God would be no less
God if he had created no world and no man' and that 'God did not
need to speak to us' (*CD* I/1, pp. 139–140). Yet his definition indicates, somewhat paradoxically, that it is God's speech to *humans* that
constitutes the essence of what it is for God to be God. The irony is
that, despite his objectivizing intent, God is defined by Barth in terms
of his relation to human religious subjectivity. He is, of course, aware
of the danger of constructing a doctrine of God in this way:

> In this light one can see how dubious it is to set the doctrine of the
> Word of God in the framework of an anthropology. In that case
> the freedom of the divine purpose for man can be asserted only at
> a later stage, while it is really denied by the starting-point. (*CD* I.1,
> p. 140)

But this is what using the concept of revelation as his theological
cornerstone has led Barth to do. He later attempted to shore up his
definition against the criticism that it was anthropologically dependent with the proposal that our knowledge of God is but a participation

in the knowledge that the triune persons have of one another (see *CD* II.1, pp. 48–49). But this is somewhat artificial. Barth has to modify radically the concept of revelation as a divine act of human salvation if he is to apply it inter-trinitarianly and in doing so he undermines the concept's original function.

THE WORD OF GOD

The central concept employed by Barth in developing his understanding of revelation is that of 'the Word of God'. His intention that this doctrine should be determinative for his whole theological system is indicated by the place he has given it as the principal subject matter of the first two-part volume of his monumental *CD*. Used by Barth, the concept 'the Word of God' refers primarily to 'God speaking', *deus dixit*. The emphasis is on an action rather than on essence or being. The Word of God is then the divine, revealing and saving event that constitutes renewed human existence. As a revelatory act, it takes a threefold form: the preaching of the Church, the written Scriptures and Jesus Christ. Only the third of these forms, Jesus Christ, is to be properly identified with its content, the Word of God, the other two are enabled in the freedom of God and in the act of revelation to become the Word of God, but they are not so in and of themselves.

The reader should not be beguiled by the simplicity with which this doctrine can be presented into supposing that understanding it is an easy matter. These polished concepts conceal an assortment of complex and baffling ideas that require careful unpacking if they are to make any sense. Let us consider then some of the notions that underlie his doctrine of the Word of God.

A determinative principle for Barth is that only God can reveal God. It means for him that God is not to be known by an examination of the created order. There is nothing of this world, no 'analogy of being', which leads or assists us, even incrementally, to gain a proper knowledge of God. It is only in the act of divine revelation and the creation of faith that believers are enabled to know him. As his theology developed, Barth affirmed that there is a correspondence, described by him as the analogy of faith, that certain objects, events and words have with God, but it is a correspondence which is bestowed on them by God in the act of revelation and which they of and in themselves do not possess.

The Word of God, as God's speech to us, encounters us in the forms of created reality. But to preserve God's freedom and absolute otherness Barth found it necessary to emphasize the distinction between these external forms and the actual content of the Word of God:

> The form is not a suitable but an unsuitable medium for God's self-presentation. It does not correspond to the matter but contradicts it. It does not unveil it but veils it . . . The place where God's Word is revealed is objectively and subjectively the cosmos in which sin reigns. The form of God's Word, then, is in fact the form of the cosmos which stands in contradiction to God. (*CD* I.1, p. 166)

It is only as Jesus Christ, the Word of God revealed, that the form is identical to the content.

The all-important question is: what does Barth here mean by 'Jesus Christ'? We saw in the previous chapter how the expressions 'the Jesus of history' and 'the biblical Christ' referred initially in Kähler's work to two competing theological perspectives of one person. Then, quite imperceptibly, they began to be used as designations for the divine and human realities that constitute that person. In Bultmann's theology the matter was further complicated by his distinction between the historical Jesus, the kerygmatic Christ and the risen Lord or eschatological saving event. What does Barth intend by 'Jesus Christ'? He clearly does not mean simply the historical figure who ministered 2,000 years ago in Galilee and Judea. This person is normally designated by Barth as Jesus of Nazareth. In fact, the relation between the Word of God and Jesus of Nazareth is for Barth a highly problematic one:

> This relation is not altered in the New Testament either. On the contrary, it is now supremely true that God conceals Himself in revealing Himself, that even and precisely in assuming form he remains free to become manifest or not to become manifest in this form. The form here is that of the *humanitas Christi*. And this brings us up against one of the hardest problems of Christology that will claim our attention more than once: Can the incarnation of the Word according to the biblical witnesses mean that the existence of the man Jesus of Nazareth was as it were in itself, in its own power and continuity, the revealing Word of God? Is the

humanitas Christi as such the revelation? Does the divine sonship of Jesus Christ mean that God's revealing has now been transmitted as it were to the existence of the man Jesus of Nazareth, that this has thus become identical with it? . . . [T]he power and continuity in which the man Jesus of Nazareth was in fact the revealed Word according to the witness of the Evangelists and apostles consisted here too in the power and continuity of the divine action in this form and not in the continuity of this form as such . . . As a matter of fact even Jesus did not become revelation to all who met Him but only to a few. (*CD* I.1, p. 323)

This extended quotation offers us one of the most illuminating insights into the christological implications of Barth's doctrine of the 'Word of God'. The existence of the man, Jesus of Nazareth is but the form of the revelation, it is not of itself the Word of God. It is, however, to be identified with the Word of God in the act of revelation but not in the continuity of its own being. Now if the Word of God constitutes the divinity of the man Jesus, we arrive at the strange outcome that Jesus of Nazareth was only divine when he was revealing, which was clearly not all the time. It is no wonder that Barth understood this as one of the hardest problems that faced his christology. Starting from where he does there appears to be no way around it.

If Jesus of Nazareth is not what Barth means by 'Jesus Christ', who or what is he referring to when he uses this expression? We indicated above how Kähler's notion of the biblical Christ was developed by Bultmann into that of the kerygmatic Christ. What began as a theological portrait of Jesus began to assume an ontological reality of its own. The kerygmatic Christ or the Christ of faith, as the proper subject of the Church's proclamation, came to be viewed as an ontological entity in some way distinct from that of Jesus of Nazareth, the figure of history. This kerygmatic Christ is the one to whom Barth normally refers when he uses the expression 'Jesus Christ'. How this 'kerygmatic' Christ differs from Jesus of Nazareth in Barth's thought can be illustrated from his discussion of the 'two states' of Christ. Reformed dogmatics had distinguished two phases in the history of Jesus – the state of humiliation and the state of exaltation, his time on earth and his time in heaven. Barth brought these together in an imaginative synthesis and argued that in the person of Christ there is a simultaneous humiliation of God and exaltation of man. Now, to someone considering the matter historically these states were clearly not simultaneous: the Son first humbled himself taking the form of a servant and a path that led to the cross; then the Father raised him from death and exalted him to his right hand. Barth's response to such a view is illuminating:

> Where and when is He not both humiliated and exalted, already exalted in His humiliation, and humiliated in His exaltation? Where in Paul for example, is he the crucified who has not yet risen, or the Risen who has not been crucified. (*CD* IV.1, p. 133)

The 'Christ' that the preacher of the Gospel and the New Testament author present to their audiences is one who is both crucified and risen, both humbled and exalted. Every New Testament title or designation is simultaneously appropriate for him. He, as the author of salvation, is present both in weakness and in power, as servant and as Lord. The Christ who is present in Church proclamation and scriptural testimony is a person who is simultaneously humbled and glorified. This is Barth's 'Jesus Christ'. But even here Barth cautions us to be careful. According to him, Jesus Christ is not to be directly identified with the preaching of the Gospel or the text of the Scriptures. Only as God graciously and sovereignly speaks to us through these forms of created reality are they identifiable with Jesus Christ. Only as the forms become God's speech to us in the act of revelation do we actually encounter the person of Jesus Christ. This is the heart of Barth's doctrine of the Word of God and the inner logic of his christological construction. What are the implications of such a christology? In particular, what does such a view indicate about the vital matter of Jesus Christ's corporality, an issue which was of such significance to the Early Church?

THE INCARNATION

We have suggested that the key to understanding the doctrine of the Word of God is to discern what Barth actually means by 'Jesus Christ'. According to him, Jesus Christ is not to be identified directly with Jesus of Nazareth, the Christ of the Bible or even the Christ of Church proclamation. These are but the creaturely forms of human flesh, text or sermon in which Jesus Christ makes himself present before the people of faith. 'For He Himself does not present Himself to them in one form but in many – indeed, He is not in Himself uniform but multiform' (*CD* IV.1, p. 763). In and of himself Jesus Christ is a unitary divine act of revelation and reconciliation. The hermeneutical power of this theory lies in its ability to integrate conceptually the whole range of christological constructs dominating early twentieth-century theological thought. For Barth these are all but the forms which 'Jesus Christ' as the eschatological saving event takes in his own divine freedom as he makes himself present to the believing community.

Barth's christological theory, as determined by his doctrine of the Word of God, is then radically different from the classical model of incarnation. Whereas he finds the unity of the various presentations of Christ in 'Jesus Christ' as a divine event, the model of incarnation finds it in 'Jesus Christ' as the person of the *incarnate* Son of God, the 'God-man'. From the perspective of an incarnation christology the 'Jesus of history', the 'biblical Christ', the 'kerygmatic Christ', *Christus Praesens* are not different ontological realities or even various forms under which the Word of God is present to the Church. They are rather all portraits, intepretations, presentations or mediations of one existent being or *hypostasis* – the incarnate Son of God, the single subject of an historical narrative that moves from Bethlehem through Calvary to the Father's right hand. In Barth's model 'Jesus Christ' refers to the divine event and not to the creaturely forms it assumes. In the incarnational model 'Jesus Christ' refers to the embodied reality. The human form cannot be abstracted from the content. The *Definition of Chalcedon* emphasizes the incarnational idea that the divine and creaturely realities are ontologically inseparable: ' . . . one and the same Christ, Son, Lord, Only-begotten, recognized in two natures, without confusion, without change, without division, without separation . . .' To speak of Jesus Christ in classical incarnation christology is to speak of a single substantial reality that always includes a human body and mind.

The difference between these two models is most apparent in the alternative explanations they offer of the contemporary presence of Christ to the believing community. For Barth Jesus Christ is immediately present to the Church in the creaturely form of flesh, text or sermon, as the direct event of salvation. For an incarnational christology Jesus Christ is not immediately present to the Church. He was born, lived, rose and ascended to the Father's right hand as an embodied reality. His presence to the Church is now one that is mediated by the Holy Spirit. 'But I tell you the truth: It is for your good that I am going away. Unless I go away, the Counsellor will not come to you . . . but when he, the Spirit of truth comes, he will guide you into all truth' (Jn 16.7,13). Within an incarnational christology the divine saving agent immediately present to the Church, as we suggested in the Chapter Ten, is not Jesus Christ but the Spirit of Christ. It is the Holy Spirit who brings the incarnate Christ and his redemptive benefits before the community of faith; who opens their eyes, ears and hearts to receive him; who unites them with him; who transforms them into his likeness, who glorifies him in their midst.

The christology derived by Barth from his conception of the Word of God, considered in itself, is quite distinct from the classical incarnational christology of the ancient Church.

JESUS CHRIST AS THE REVEALER OF GOD

In considering the different elements making up the structure of Barth's doctrine of the Word of God we come finally to the foundational idea that in revealing God, Jesus Christ is himself divine:

> [T]he statement about Christ's deity is to be understood in the sense that Christ reveals His Father. But this Father of His is God. He who reveals Him, then, reveals God. But who can reveal God except God Himself? . . . Now the Christ who reveals the Father is also a creature and His work is a creaturely work. But if He were only a creature he could not reveal God, for the creature certainly cannot take God's place and work in His place. If He reveals God, then irrespective of His creaturehood He Himself has to be God, And since this is a case of either/or, He has to be full and true God without reduction or limitation, without more or less. Any such restriction would not merely weaken His deity; it would deny it. To confess Him as the revelation of His Father is to confess Him as essentially equal in deity with this Father of His. (*CD* I.1, p. 406)

This has been widely recognized as an important argument for the divinity of Christ. Wolfhart Pannenberg maintains that: 'The demonstration of the connection of Jesus' divinity with the concept of revelation constitutes one of Barth's greatest theological contributions.'[39] Let us, however, examine the idea of revelation suggested here a little more closely. Consider the opening sentence of the letter to the Hebrews: 'In the past God spoke to our forefathers through the prophets at many times and in various ways, but in these last days he has spoken to us by his Son (Heb. 1.1). How are we to understand God's revelation of himself to Israel through the words of the prophets? If these were indeed events of divine revelation, then by what divine power were they effected? The general testimony of the Scriptures is that the prophets spoke through the inspiration of the Holy Spirit. What does a revelatory event of this sort tell us about the ontological status of the prophet? That a person reveals God clearly does not imply that he or she is in any measure divine, it merely indicates that they have been empowered by the Holy Spirit of God to be the bearer of God's word. Why should it be any different with Jesus? The Hebrews text quoted above indicates that Jesus differed from the prophets of old not because of the nature of his revelatory action but because of his person. He was God's Son. It can be argued quite plausibly that Jesus' own prophetic ministry was enabled or empowered by the Holy Spirit. Luke records Jesus as quoting from Isaiah when he read the Scriptures in the synagogue in his home town: 'The Spirit of the Lord is on me, because he has anointed me to preach good news to the poor' (Lk. 4.18a). If this is the case Jesus' revelation of God is of itself no more than an indication that he was anointed by the Spirit. According to John's Gospel the unique feature of Jesus' revelation is that he came from the Father and that he was one with the Father. The relation of the Son to the Father determines the status of the revelation rather than the other way round.

We are suggesting then that Jesus' revelatory ministry does not of itself, without consideration of his particular relation to the Father, provide evidence for his divine being. All that it immediately indicates is the revelatory presence of the Holy Spirit on his person.

CONCLUSION

The question that has been of concern to us both in this chapter and the book as a whole is that of the relation between the divine and human realities of Christ. In early twentieth-century theology this age-old question was transposed into one about the relation between Jesus of Nazareth, the Christ of Church proclamation and Jesus Christ as the divine saving or revelatory event. Barth's considered response to this question of the relation between these christological concepts is his doctrine of the Word of God. We have offered a brief exposition of this doctrine along with a critique of its structures, suggesting a number of reasons why they struggle to bear the weight of a coherent body of Christian doctrine.

First, Barth's idea of revelation as an event in contemporary human religious consciousness is too anthropologically dependent to serve as the primary concept for the divine essence. Put bluntly, God's existence does not depend on his saving revelation to humans. Second, his understanding of the relation of the Word of God to Jesus of Nazareth as a continuity of action rather than as a continuity of being was recognized by Barth himself to be highly problematic. It indicates Jesus' divinity is an outcome of his revealing action rather than an aspect of his being and is consequently discontinuous. Third, the theory that Jesus Christ is a divine act that takes the form of flesh, text or sermon is unable to affirm the indissoluble union of the divine Word with human being. Finally, the argument that Jesus' revelatory ministry established his divinity does not stand up to careful examination. In short, although the doctrine of the Word of God is a testimony to the imaginative brilliance of its architect, its significant structural deficiencies preclude it from serving as an effective bridge between the epistemological concerns of modernity and the ancient dogma of the Church. His attempt to reinvent the discipline of Christian theology made it impossible for him to faithfully reiterate what had been said before.

Barth's christology also brought to completion the project initiated by Martin Kähler to explain how Christ as the object of Christian faith is significantly different from the person that historical-critical scholarship described as the Jesus of history. Many in the theological world, however, were not satisfied that this whole undertaking had treated with due seriousness the religious significance of the life of Jesus as disclosed in the Gospels. This concern led a number of theologians to develop their own interpretations of the person of Jesus as they attempted to redress this perceived weakness. Günther Bornkamm, Edward Shillebeeckx and Ernst Käsemann were among those who believed it was appropriate to try again to provide a critical historical account of the life of Jesus. A common feature of their work was the conviction that the historical life of Jesus as we uncover it in the Gospels, embedded in the culture of his age, is a more faithful starting point for christology than theological reflection on the nature of the triune God. Wolfhart Pannenberg is of particular interest in that he sought to combine this commitment to Jesus' history with Barth's theory of divine self-revelation so that he might offer a historically robust explanation of the person of Christ. We will evaluate the success of his project in Chapter Twelve.

RESURRECTION AS REVELATION

WOLFHART PANNENBERG (b. 1928)

Pannenberg is a Lutheran systematic theologian who places particular emphasis on the historical development of dogma. It means that he treats the theological tradition with great seriousness, seeking both to understand it and to explain why at certain junctures he is compelled to diverge from it. In particular, he gives a careful account of why modern christology is unable to follow the historic Church in using a doctrine of incarnation to explain the person of Jesus. Pannenberg also offers a significant corrective to Barth's interpretation of Jesus Christ, but here his aim is to modify rather than replace his theological framework and he continues to rely on Barth's concept of revelation to explain both the divinity of Christ and the essence of God. Let us examine Pannenberg's adaptation of Barth's christology and see whether it does in fact enable him to give an adequate explanation of the relation of the divine and human in Jesus Christ.

CHRISTOLOGY FROM BELOW

Pannenberg believed that all christological interpretation has as its starting point the historical person of Jesus, the underlying reality that is the ground of all our theological conceptions of his being. He argued that we need to penetrate behind the message of the apostles, which includes the presentation of Jesus found in the Gospels, to come to this person as he is in himself, without theological interpretation:

> For this purpose dogmatic Christology must go behind the New Testament to the base to which it points and which supports faith

in Jesus, that is to the history of Jesus. Christology has to ask and show the extent to which this history substantiates faith in Jesus. (*Jesus – God and Man* p. 29)[40]

Starting from the historic person of Jesus, we can observe how the Church's christological concepts came to be developed:

> Jesus' titles of honour and their history – the Kyrios title shows it more clearly – were influenced by the development of the history of religions prior to and in the environment of the young church. It is valid to determine the legitimate Christian sense of those titles, the essential Christian meaning that their use intended to express, but which is perhaps not bound to them. (pp. 24–25)

Christology must then be able to stand up to historical scrutiny. We need, for instance, to be able to explain why the title Messiah or Christ 'expresses the connection between Jesus' activity and fate and Israel's eschatological expectation' (p. 32). If there is no such historically grounded relation between them then the title is falsely used and our interpretation of Jesus unfounded. It was Pannenberg's argument that this process of historical development 'in the course of which the unity of the man Jesus with God became recognized, runs counter to the kind of concepts that speak of God's becoming man' (p. 33). And this is the underlying problem with the idea that the pre-existing Logos assumed a human nature – it moves in the wrong direction. Such a doctrine presupposes the divinity of Jesus. But 'we must first enquire about how Jesus' appearance in history led to the recognition of his divinity' (p. 34).

Pannenberg recognizes a similar problem when christology is shaped by the requirements of soteriology. Again, it is the history of Jesus rather than his redemptive significance that must determine christological interpretation. 'Jesus possesses significance "for us" only to the extent that this significance is inherent in himself, in his history and in his person constituted by that history' (p. 48). In short, Pannenberg is insistent that the history of Jesus of Nazareth is formative for all christological construction. This is where it must begin. The historical Jesus is the foundation of our christological concepts and it is against the events of his life that they are to be measured and adjudged. Let us see then how he applies this principle to the idea of divine self-revelation, the determinative theological concept in the christology of Karl Barth.

REVELATION AS RESURRECTION

Barth's christology found its primary location not in the life of Jesus, but in the divine revelatory act, a contemporary event in human religious consciousness, albeit with past and future dimensions. Although Pannenberg, believes that Barth's idea of revelation is necessary for a modern conceptualization of Jesus' divinity, he understands the revelatory event to be located not in our subjective religious experience but in the actual history of Jesus. And within that history he holds that it is Jesus' bodily resurrection that constitutes the one, definitive act of God's self-revelation. This is a theological step with far-reaching implications. We suggested in the previous chapter that one weakness of Barth's idea of understanding God in terms self-revelation was its anthropological determination. By shifting the divine revelatory event from the arena of contemporary private experience to a public historical occurrence, Pannenberg has given it a status that is quite independent of human self-consciousness. The tomb is empty whether or not anyone observed it. Revelation is now identified directly with an objective occurrence in the life of Jesus of Nazareth rather than with an inner spiritual event in human experience. Further, Pannenberg argues with great originality that it is the event of the resurrection that actually constitutes the divinity of Jesus. Let us follow the steps that lead him to this conclusion.

In the context of contemporary Jewish expectation the resurrection of Jesus had a particular significance. '[I]n all probability the earthly Jesus' expectation was not directed toward, so to speak, a privately experienced resurrection from the dead but toward the imminent universal resurrection of the dead, which would, of course, include himself should his death precede it' (*Jesus – God and Man*, p. 66). Thus, when confronted with Jesus' resurrection his disciples viewed it 'as the beginning of the universal resurrection of the dead, as the beginning of the events of the end of history' (p. 66). As a result, the resurrection of Jesus is, in the context of Jewish expectation, not a random occurrence open to arbitrary interpretation. It has rather a series of inescapable theological implications:

a) If Jesus has been raised then the end of the world has begun.
b) If Jesus has been raised, this for a Jew can only mean that God himself has confirmed the pre-Easter activity of Jesus.

c) Through his resurrection from the dead, Jesus moved so close to the Son of Man that the insight became obvious: the Son of Man is none other than the man Jesus who will come again.

d) If Jesus, having been raised from the dead, is ascended to God and thereby if the end of the world has begun, then God is ultimately revealed in Jesus. (*Jesus – God and Man*, pp. 66–69)

We should take notice of what has happened here. Pannenberg has grounded the Church's knowledge of Jesus divinity, not in the believing individual's personal salvific experience but in the community of faith and its shared understanding of God's saving purpose in history. It is a robust argument which finds support from what we know of the high status that the earliest Church uniformly ascribed to Jesus after the resurrection. Pannenberg, however, differs from that community in his interpretation of the divinity that came to be ascribed to Jesus. He writes:

If these apocalyptic ideas are translated into Hellenistic terminology and conceptuality, there meaning is: in Jesus God himself has appeared on earth. God himself – or God's revelatory figure, the Logos, the Son – has been among us as a man in the figure of Jesus. In this sense, in the transition of the Palestinian tradition into the Syrian sphere eschatology was translated throughout into epiphany. (p. 68)

Pannenberg is acutely aware of how a modern interpretation of the divinity of Christ in terms of revelation differs from that of the early Church. Faced with the reality of the risen Jesus as a person worthy of divine honour, the first Christians held him to be the incarnation of a previously existing divine being – the Logos or the Son of God who had come to dwell among them from the Father's side. This is not, according to Pannenberg, an interpretation that is acceptable to modernity:

But can these concepts be anything more for us today than mythical pictures? In the age of technology can we speak seriously of the descent and ascent of a heavenly divine being? . . . This constitutes the mythical element of the incarnational Christology: it conceptually divides the eternal Son of God and the earthly, human appearance of Jesus, which together constitute the concrete existence of Jesus, into two separate beings. (p. 154)

Although Barth's doctrine of the Word of God is also quite different from a classical doctrine of incarnation (see Chapter Eleven), the structural distinctions between them is a matter to which he was careful not to draw close attention. Pannenberg, however, is far more open in explaining why a modern, 'revelatory' christology is, to his mind, a more adequate alternative to the doctrine of incarnation as an interpretation of the person of Jesus. Two of the objections that he raises against an incarnational christology are its mythological Hellenistic form and its understanding of Jesus as the union of two distinct beings. Our immediate focus at this point is not on the reasons for his rejection of the idea of incarnation. It is rather on the adequacy of the concept of 'revelation' to replace incarnation as the principal building block for christological construction.

THE DIVINITY OF JESUS AS RESURRECTION

Having offered a robust defence for the physical resurrection of Jesus, Pannenberg details the logical steps that lead from the factuality of this event to our understanding of the divinity of his person:

a) The Christ event is God's revelation . . . only to the extent that it brings the beginning of the end of all things.
b) The concept of self-revelation includes the fact that there can be only a single revelation.
c) The concept of God's self-revelation contains the idea that the Revealer and what is revealed is identical. (p. 129)

Pannenberg acknowledges that his own position is dependent on Barth's doctrine of God's self-revelation. And he uses this doctrine as a hermeneutical tool to explain why Jesus is divine. But what is the status of this explanatory tool? Barth's standing in twentieth-century dogmatic theology means that Pannenberg is able to present these elements of his argument with the assurance of one who is not expecting to be challenged. The question of their status remains. They are not of themselves intuitively obvious. I, for one, can find no compelling reason why any of the assertions above is in fact true. They are certainly not generated from a study of the history of Jesus or of Jewish messianic expectation. Rather, as Pannenberg concedes, the historical origin of these ideas lies closer to hand: 'The exclusive use of the concept of revelation for God's self-disclosure goes back to German Idealism, especially to Hegel' (p. 127). The point is that Pannenberg, like the early Christians, is compelled to use an interpretive tool to explain the divinity of Jesus that is not derived immediately from an analysis of his history. This raises the question of whether it is actually possible to construct a high christology entirely from below. However, if we are to read Pannenberg sympathetically we must assume, for the time being, that Barth's doctrine of divine self-revelation has been established as theologically successful and that it is appropriate for Pannenberg to use it for his own project. And it is with that assumption, or suspension of disbelief, that we continue with his presentation.

The principle that the Revealer and the matter revealed is identical means that in his resurrection, that is, the primal act of divine self-revelation, Jesus is himself identical with the essence of God. Jesus is personally divine. The resurrection is then ontologically and not just noetically constitutive for Jesus' divinity:

> [O]ne must keep clearly in mind today that the divine-human unity of Jesus can never be expressed independently of the Easter event . . . Jesus' resurrection is not only constitutive for our perception of his divinity, but it is ontologically constitutive for that divinity. Apart from the resurrection from the dead, Jesus would not be God, even though from the perspective of the resurrection, he is retrospectively one with God in his whole pre-Easter life. (p. 224)

In historical theology the notion that at some stage in his career Jesus became the divine Son of God is considered to belong to the heresy described as Adoptionism – the view that Jesus was adopted into divine Sonship rather than possessing such status intrinsically. In part answer to this objection Pannenberg argues that prior to the events of Easter Jesus was proleptically or anticipatively divine:

> To this extent the resurrection event has retroactive power. Jesus did not simply become something that he previously had not been, but his pre-Easter claim was confirmed by God. (p. 135)

For Pannenberg, the claims to authority that Jesus made in his preaching could only be verified in the future judgement of the Son of Man. It was because Jesus was to be resurrected as the coming Son of Man that he was able to speak and act authoritatively in his earthly ministry. There was then an historical openness about his authority and status. It is in this sense that his public pre-Easter ministry anticipated his divine becoming. Nevertheless, the revelatory act, the identification of Jesus with the essence of God only occurs at the end of his career.

THE RELATION OF THE DIVINE AND HUMAN IN THE CONSCIOUSNESS OF JESUS

Although Pannenberg finds the grounds for the divinity of Jesus in the resurrection event, he believes that there must be evidence of this 'identification with the divine essence' in Jesus' religious consciousness:

> If the pre-Easter Jesus had not been related at all to his unity with God in his self-consciousness, then – assuming that we may presuppose this unity as confirmed on other grounds – he would not be one with himself and to that extent not one with God. (p. 326)

Pannenberg holds that Jesus' divinity must in some way impinge on his self-consciousness. Although he does not believe that Jesus applied to himself any Messianic titles, he argues that he was 'one with God through his dedication to the Father . . . Such personal community is at the same time essential community' (p. 336). The weakness in this argument is that although Jesus understood himself to have a unique relation with God, there was for him always an absolute distinction between his own ego and that of God. Put crudely the problem is: 'How can Jesus be God if he knows himself to be distinct from God?' Pannenberg recognizes the difficulty and argues that Jesus is to be identified not with God the Father, but with God the Son. But how are we able to speak of Jesus' identity relation with the Son if his historical consciousness indicates only a relation with the Father?

> Jesus' self-consciousness has shown him to be related to God, to be sure, not directly to 'the Logos' as the second Person of the Trinity, but to the Heavenly Father. (p. 334)

Jesus' unity with God has consequently to be explained dialectically. In his personal communion with God and dedication to him Jesus 'shows himself identical with the correlate Son already implied in the understanding of God as the Father, the Son whose characteristic is not to exist on the basis of his own resources but wholly from the Father' (p. 336). Jesus' divinity is consequently established indirectly. His absolute dependence on God shows him to be identical with the second person of the Trinity, the one who himself exists in a dependent relation to the Father. The conclusion is that because the second person of the Trinity is divine Jesus is himself divine. But this is not an argument that Pannenberg's theological structure allows him to make.

Pannenberg's christological project is clearly defined. He wants to construct a christology based on the history of Jesus and to do so he believes it is necessary to replace the concept of the incarnation of the Logos with that of divine self-revelation. He argues that: 'Today the idea of revelation must take the place of the Logos concept as the point of departure for Christology' (p. 168). There is then for Pannenberg no Logos or eternal Son that can be conceptually distinguished from Jesus of Nazareth. Odd though it may appear, the second person of the Trinity is for him simply the historical Jesus:

> If Jesus' history and his person now belong to the essence, to the divinity of God, then the distinction that Jesus maintained between himself and the Father also belongs to the divinity of God. (p. 159)

But if this is the case to identify Jesus with the second person of the Trinity is to say nothing new about him. The Logos is not within his theological framework a third term, a conceptually distinct divine entity that can be used dialectically along with that of the Father to explain Jesus' relation with God. In short, Pannenberg can have no recourse to trinitarian ideas like that of divine Sonship that have been derived from an incarnational christology. Jesus' divinity cannot then be established by identifying him with the second person of the Trinity. Encapsulated here is the problem Pannenberg has in saying anything of substance about Jesus' divinity other than that he was raised from the dead. He is far more at ease in highlighting perceived weaknesses in the tradition's use of the doctrine of incarnation than he is in developing an alternative model to explain the relation of the divine and human in Jesus.

CONCLUSION

Pannenberg's exposition raises two questions of far-reaching significance for theology. 'Can christology be done from below?' and 'Is the concept of revelation a more effective building block for christology than that of the incarnation of the Logos?' Let us consider them both in turn.

First, Pannenberg's project is to construct his christology only from material that can be derived from the historic life of Jesus. He argues, however, that the events of that life must be interpreted in the context of contemporary Jewish apocalyptic expectation. This is the hermeneutical structure that determines their meaning. The theological concepts of the contemporary Jewish faith-system are consequently accepted by him as they stand. No questions are raised about either their derivation or development. What Pannenberg is not willing to accept is the interpretive framework provided by the first Christians, one which recognized Jesus as the divine Son who was sent into the world by the Father as the Logos who became flesh or as the one equal to God who humbled himself and took human form. This arbitrary privileging of Jewish apocalyptic theology draws our attention to Pannenberg's own dependence on certain *a priori* theological concepts in his christological construction, concepts which are not themselves derived from the life of Jesus. We also saw above how Pannenberg was dependent on Barth's doctrine of divine self-revelation to explain Jesus' divinity. It would seem that if we are to interpret Jesus meaningfully as the proper object of Christian faith we must have recourse to some transcendental interpretive scheme. And if 'a christology from below' does not admit the use of such a hermeneutical framework it can surely be no more than a mundane exercise. If, however, this principle requires only that our christological formulations are to be consistent with what can be known of the historical Jesus then it is certainly a legitimate rule.

Second, Pannenberg's desire to replace the incarnation of the Logos with a more acceptable theory is one that is shared by many. Ever since the Socinian challenge to the dogma of the Nicene Creed in the sixteenth century there has been a concern within modernity that the doctrine of the incarnation is an inadequate tool to express the relation of the divine and human in Jesus Christ. Consequently, the attempt to discover a new way to conceptualize this relation has engaged the imagination of a multitude of theologians for the past 100 years. They have considered replacing the supposedly static qualities suggested by the natures of Christ with dynamic ones; transposing ideas of substance into those of relation; using Jewish rather than Greek forms of conceptuality; favouring the category of action over that of being and re-imagining the christological question within the frameworks of personality or morality. The difficulty that all such projects face is that the concept of incarnation along with its related ideas is integral to the architecture of Christian theology. The building cannot stand without it. The historic doctrines of the Trinity, Christ, the Spirit and creation are all dependent on it. The notion that we can replace a doctrine of incarnation and still make use of classical trinitarian concepts is mistaken. Pannenberg's attempt to explain Jesus' divinity in terms of his relation to the second person of the Trinity is but one example of a common but surprising failure to recognize that such concepts are derived directly from a theology of incarnation. To remove the idea of incarnation from the theology of the Church is like trying to remove the bones from a body – the whole structure collapses.

If modern christology is to enter again into genuine conversation with the historic faith of the Church it will need to re-appropriate the doctrine of the incarnation. No other way has been found to work.

CONCLUSION

CHAPTER THIRTEEN

AN ECUMENICAL CHRISTOLOGY

We have considered the work of a number of significant theologians ancient and modern in this potted survey of 2,000 years of christological reflection. They fall naturally into two sections: classical and modern christology. Classical christology is, broadly speaking, the Church's shared interpretation of Jesus encapsulated in the Nicene Creed and the *Definition of Chalcedon*. We described it earlier as the publicly articulated set of beliefs about the person of Jesus Christ as true God and true man, conceived as the eternal Son of God incarnated as a human being for our salvation. As we have seen, this interpretive theory evolved into its present form over a considerable period of time. Each modification served to explain or qualify a view to which the Church had already given its support. The intention was always that the resultant conception of Jesus should receive universal assent. In practice the credal formulae of classical christology have served as the most effective unifying symbols of the universal Church, Orthodox, Catholic and Protestant.

In contrast, modern christology is the open and many faceted pattern of christological conversation that is marked by a clear breach with the classical model and the settlements achieved at Nicea and Chalcedon. A common feature of this fluid discussion about the person of Jesus is its criticism of traditional christological formulations, challenging both their coherence and their metaphysical presuppositions. This has meant that modern christology has been, at least to begin with, iconoclastic in intention. It sought to pull down the theological structures of an earlier age. More recently there have been within it a number of imaginative attempts to rebuild an interpretive theory of Jesus which can be of service to the worshipping Church. In our study we have considered some of the most significant of these and highlighted the structural deficiencies which have limited their success. Further, modern christology has generally lacked a corporate or ecumenical vision. Its culture of intellectual independency has meant that the constructive insights of its leading theologians have often been undermined by their own disciples rather than being developed by them into a widely supported confessional theology. Consequently, after 450 years modern christology has not been able to provide the Church with an interpretation of Jesus that can account for his role as both the object of its worship and the paradigm of its life and that is able to serve as a unifying instrument of the wider Christian community.

Given all this, why do 'modern' Christians not simply return to the more robust and secure world of classical christology for their interpretation of Jesus? One reason is that the nexus of ideas and attitudes, now described as the European Enlightenment, has raised a host of unsettling questions in the minds of those of us who have lived under its sway. We feel unable, with intellectual integrity, to simply shut out such questions and pretend that they had never been asked. Consequently, a conceptual bridge needs to be constructed if the prodigal sons and daughters of modernity are to traverse the intellectual gap that exists between them and the orthodox tradition and so relate meaningfully with the Fathers of the Church. In this final chapter I will outline some of the characteristics, suggested by this survey, that are required of a christology that is to serve as such a bridge.

A GENEROUS ORTHODOXY

Responsible christological formation must have an eye to the wider Church. To develop a metaphor used earlier in our study, the christological project is like the construction of a very large jigsaw puzzle on the dining-room table in which the extended family has for some time been participating. The gifted but self-centred child who breaks up the entire puzzle one morning so that he can start all over again on his own without any obfuscating input from his older relatives or competing siblings has failed to recognize the corporate and complex nature of the enterprise. There is, in short, no place in an ecumenical christology for the hubris of the theologian who would begin theology completely afresh without regard for the tradition of the Church. Neither is there room for those who, looking only to antiquity, would close their minds to the insights gained from modern theological discussion. A host of Christians have imaginatively sought to find ways of presenting the Gospel with integrity in the context of the philosophical and hermeneutical questions of this age and we must approach their work in a spirit of generosity. Christology needs to be practised with a degree of humility, a willingness to recognize the significant accomplishments of both the ancient and the more recent past and to build on them with both care and responsibility.

AN EPISTEMOLOGY OF THE DIVINITY OF JESUS

The most pressing question that has faced christological thought in modern times has to do with our knowledge of Jesus' divinity. In an epistemological climate dominated by the constraints of empiricism Christians have struggled to explain how it is that they know Jesus of Nazareth to be more than a man. Pannenberg's thesis that the Church came to recognize the divinity of Jesus in the event of his resurrection as it is interpreted in the context of Jewish eschatological expectation is historically robust. There is strong evidence to support the view that it was soon after his resurrection that the first Christians began to afford Jesus the status of a divine being in their prayers, greetings, benedictions and worship. Pannenberg's argument holds true even if one interprets the resurrection, ascension and pouring out of the Spirit on the Church as a disclosure of Jesus' divine being, rather than by claiming, as he does, that the resurrection is the single revelatory event that constituted it. The particular value of his approach is that it grounds a Christian recognition of Jesus' status in the events of his history as they are interpreted within the theological framework of the worshipping community.

Pannenberg's exposition, however, fails to give a satisfactory account of the personal or existential dimension of the knowledge of Jesus' divinity. The historical data of Jesus' life interpreted theologically do not of themselves compel assent. Not every practising Jew who heard about the resurrection believed that Jesus was the Son of God. This is sufficient uncertainty in any historical event for the sceptic to take secure refuge. To know truly who Jesus is there must be an occasion of divine disclosure in the human religious consciousness. Forsyth expressed this event in terms of the believer's experience of salvation. In a parallel approach Barth explained it as a divine revelatory event. His maxim that only God can reveal God is a timely reminder of our human dependence on the generous self-disclosing action of God if we are to know anything at all about the divine reality of Christ. This revelatory act should not be understood as the provision of new information. It is, rather, that enlightening action of God which brings the believer to an assured conviction of the truth of the interpreted events of Jesus' history presented in the Gospel.

The mistake of much twentieth-century theology has been to identify this divine event of salvation or revelation with Jesus Christ rather than with the Holy Spirit. It is the Holy Spirit who lifts the veil which restricts the sight, softens the hardened hearts and opens the closed minds of the hearers of the Gospel so that they might know the truth about Jesus. As Jesus through his person and public ministry disclosed the nature of his Father, so the Spirit of Christ now, through the preaching of the Gospel, discloses to the eye of faith the true status of the Son. The force of Barth's emphasis on God's sovereign freedom in revelation and salvation loses nothing of import and has much to gain in relating our theological reflection to the orthodox tradition and to the perspective of the biblical authors if such divine revelatory action is interpreted pneumatologically rather than christologically.

It was Bultmann who most clearly emphasized the subject element in our knowledge of Jesus as divine. The objective nature of divine revelation must not obscure the secondary, but closely related subjective act of existential trust and commitment in the personal attainment of such knowledge. It is in God-given faith that we come to know truly who Jesus is.

From our survey we come then to learn that there are four linked realities that mediate to us our knowledge of Jesus as divine, each of them requiring its own proper emphasis. These are: the public, historical events of Jesus' life, death and resurrection along with the outpouring of the Spirit; the community of faith in which those events are witnessed and interpreted and into which the believer is incorporated; the divine revelatory and salvific action of the Holy Spirit in human consciousness; and the individual's existential response of trusting faith in the Father's promise of salvation made known in the proclamation of the Gospel.

A DEFENCE OF THE FULL HUMANITY OF JESUS

The movement that sought to discover the historical Jesus using the methods of modern historiography met, as we have seen, with mixed success. The person it claimed to uncover often bore an uncanny resemblance to the spirituality of the investigators and to their highest ideals or, in the case of Schweitzer's study, was so radically out of step with current religious sensibility that there did not seem to be any point in pursuing the matter. Kähler rightly recognized that the person it portrayed could have no significant impact on history. A Jesus such as this certainly could not serve as the proper object of Christian faith and worship. This outcome of the historical examination of Jesus' life was probably to be expected. Any incident or interpretive insight in the Gospel narratives that indicated a relation of the divine and human in Jesus was excluded from the relevant data on methodological grounds. Modern historiography simply does not have within itself the resources to deal with questions of divine being or action.

The movement did, however, offer from its study of the Synoptic Gospels some persuasive outlines of Jesus as a man whose mission and consequent actions could be explained within the religious expectations and historical conditions of his time. What are we to make of these accounts of Jesus? It has been the practice of much modern theology to discard them, not because such portraits lacked historical foundation but because they are considered religiously insignificant or irrelevant. And so there has arisen in modern times a tendency to disjoin theology from history, dogmatics from the study of the Gospels and other contemporary religious texts. But this unhelpful lack of intellectual integration is surely the outcome of a christological error, a failure to properly affirm the theological significance of the human life of Jesus?[41] Are these portraits of Jesus, at their best, not authentic sketches of Jesus' humanity? In order to answer this there are a number of other questions that we first need to consider. Did Jesus have a life that was continuous with our own, subject as we are to suffering and daily temptation as he sought to be faithful to God's calling? Is the account of his sufferings, as we find it recorded in the Gospels, primarily the story of a man standing faithfully before his God experiencing great spiritual anguish and a deep sense of personal dereliction? In short, was Jesus in possession of a human consciousness, with human thought processes and a full range of human emotions? And if he was, is the working of such a mind open to normal historical investigation? We have suggested in our study that the answer to all of these questions is 'yes'. The historian does have theoretical access to the human life of Jesus and is restricted in his or her investigations of it more by the limitations of the sources than by any *a priori* theological principles.

In the sixteenth century the Socinians argued that the Gospels portrayed Jesus as a man dependent on God, who sought the Father's help in prayer and who was personally empowered by the Holy Spirit. And in this matter, although not in the implications they drew from it, they were absolutely right. The incipient Apollinarianism which attempts to safeguard the divinity of Christ by denying the integrity of the human mind of Jesus is out of step not only with the historical and biblical concerns of modernity but also with the Chalcedonian settlement of orthodox theology. An ecumenical christology is required, as Christians have recognized from the beginning, to defend the full humanity of Jesus. It must be willing to affirm that he was a man dependent on the Spirit, urgent in personal prayer as he battled against temptation, whose words and actions were shaped by the religion and culture of his time.

AN AFFIRMATION OF BOTH THE DIVINE AND HUMAN IN JESUS

A common critique of classical christology has to do with its doctrine of the two natures of Christ. The concern is that this is a particularly Greek, as opposed to Hebrew, concept and that it is far too static or mechanistic to describe the dynamic personality of Jesus. Such an objection, however, completely misses the point. The issue is not about how nature is defined but how Jesus might be spoken of as both truly divine and truly human: how he is both the proper object of Christian faith and worship and yet a human being, just as we are, with a human physiology and a human consciousness who experienced joy and pain as we do. The task of christology remains the same as it ever was: the provision of a coherent conceptual and theological explanation of Jesus' person as both divine and human. In the post-Chalcedonian discussion the expression 'the divine and human *realities*' of Christ was sometimes used. This is but one indication that the argument was not about the interpretation of a specific Greek term. A bridging-christology does not then have to commit itself to a classical metaphysic in its interpretation of Christ, but it is required to give an account of how this person is ontologically one with both the Creator and the creature. The Arian debate brought a degree of clarity to this matter. It established that the relation of Jesus to God cannot be explained in merely functional terms.

Jesus is not divine because he obeyed the will of the Father, or because he was appointed by God to a particular office. Conversely, he is not a human merely because he acts like one of us. Rather his unity both with the Father and with humankind is a matter of who he is and not simply what he does. It has to do with his person, his being.

To affirm that Jesus had a human consciousness is not then to deny that he is also truly divine. In the fourth century the Church rejected Apollinarianism but remained true to the decisions of Nicea and the affirmation that Jesus Christ was ontologically one with God. Today we need to affirm that the life of Jesus is open to scientific, historical research but deny that this discipline can of itself offer an adequate account of his person. We must insist with the Socinians that Jesus was a man wholly dependent on the Holy Spirit in every aspect of his life but deny that this precludes him from being the eternal Son of God made flesh. The tradition has within itself the theological resources to integrate these two perspectives in a coherent way.[42] In short, an ecumenical christology must affirm both history and theology. It must insist that Jesus is truly one of us and that he nevertheless remains the eternal Son of God.

AN INTEGRATED PERSONALITY

Another widely expressed concern with a Chalcedonian christology is that it suggests a schizophrenic personality. It is asked: 'What would a psychiatrist make of a person who was both divine and human?' This is a helpful question in that it takes us right to the heart of the christological discussion. If Jesus was, so to speak, on the ancient psychiatrist's couch, the analyst would have no natural access to his divine being, for such knowledge comes, as we have learnt, only by divine disclosure. He or she would be confronted with a human personality that is, in principle, continuous with any other. There would be no christological reason to diagnose any form of psychosis. The analyst might of course be somewhat disturbed by the authority with which the subject spoke; or with the predications he offered of the fateful outcome of his own mission; or with his personal conviction in his own unique relation to God; or even perhaps with his tendency to refer to himself as the apocalyptic Son of Man. If the analyst was a religious Jew he might well have thought Jesus to be a blasphemer or hopelessly self-deluded. The Gospels indicate that this was not an uncommon assessment of him by his contemporaries.

Nevertheless there is nothing in all of these phenomena which is of itself inconsistent with Jesus possessing an integrated human personality. Rather, in his trusting dependence on God, his clear sense of mission, his moral courage and his loving service to others, he exhibited the most truly integrated human personality that we can imagine.

When we speak of Jesus' divinity, however, we need to remind ourselves that we are not referring to a reality which is in some way equivalent or comparable to that of his humanity. In this matter we are totally out of our depth. Psychology has no access at all into the working of the divine mind. When by God's self-revealing grace the divine being of Christ is made known to us we can do no more than fall prostrate before him and offer to him our heartfelt worship and unconditional obedience. It is at that moment that we recognize that we have here to do with the one eternal God who dwells in unapproachable light. The prophet's word of caution is appropriate: 'Let all the earth be silent before him.' And yet it is the faith of the Church that the events of Jesus' life and death can be understood also as the decision of a divine will, one that did not count equality with God something to be grasped, but rather chose to humble himself by taking human form and giving himself up on our behalf. The classical affirmation by the Church of both a divine and a human volition in Christ does not indicate some sort of divine/human amalgam or psychotic confusion in his psyche. The incarnate Son of God has, as was argued above, an integrated human personality, but he also continues to exercise at all times in his own absolute freedom a divine choosing, a sovereign volition, the outworking of which can be known to us only by faith and only in small part. For 'who has known the mind of the Lord?'

A DOCTRINE OF INCARNATION

There are a number of ways that the relation of the divine and human in Jesus has been interpreted, both in the Scriptures and in the history of christological discussion. The New Testament theologians: John, Paul and the author of the letter to the Hebrews each recognized Jesus to be the presence in human form of a previously existing divine being. When in the second century the Church found that it was being overwhelmed by the teaching of Gnosticism, it emphasized the doctrine of the incarnation of the divine Son so as to safeguard the goodness of earthly existence and the role of the supreme God as creator of this world. In the Arian debate, the doctrine of the incarnation was the theological structure within which the concept of homoousion was proposed. Jesus Christ as the incarnation of the eternal Son was held to be of the 'same essence' as the Father. This idea of a 'oneness of being' was later applied to the Holy Spirit and so went on to form the conceptual framework for the doctrine of the Trinity. Incarnation thus became the supporting foundation for the principal doctrines of Christian theology.

Modern Christology is to a large extent the outworking of the concerted attack by the Socinians on the doctrine of the incarnation in the sixteenth century. Since then it has found it extremely difficult to come to terms with this concept. Bultmann and Pannenberg both considered the incarnation to be a mythological explanation of Jesus' divinity devised by the earliest Christian community. Barth's interpretation of Jesus Christ as God's self-revelation is the most thoroughgoing attempt in recent times to provide a conceptual alternative to it. We have indicated why his understanding of Jesus Christ as a divine act taking various creaturely forms is not, however, a theologically viable option. Further, a coherent doctrine of the Trinity requires that the Word of God is not merely, as the Arians argued, a divine action – God's speech to us – he is, as the eternal Son, a self-subsisting personal reality of the same essence as the Father. The account of this Son coming into the world; or being sent to us by the Father; or returning to heaven; or humbling himself and taking human form; or becoming like us in every way, might suggest to some the language of myth. But it is difficult to understand why. Is a trinitarian interpretation of God, constructed as it is from a doctrine of incarnation, more mythological than a monistic understanding of him? Is it more difficult for faith to conceive of Jesus as the incarnation of a divine person than to view him as the embodiment of a revelatory event?

It is the argument of the tradition that the eternal Son of God assumed to himself a human nature. This means that the human personality of Jesus has no independent existence. In theological terms it is 'anhypostatic'. It exists only and always as the human personality of the incarnated Son of God. In the incarnation of the Son it has its being, in technical language, it is 'enhypostasised'.[43] This is why the person or *hypostasis* of Jesus Christ is but one indivisible reality. Yet his complete deity and true humanity are not thereby mixed or confused, rather each continues to exhibit its own proper characteristics as the characteristics of the one person, the incarnate Son of God.

If an ecumenical christology is to serve as a bridge which will enable moderns to re-engage positively with this theological tradition of the Church and with the christological concepts of the New Testament authors it will need to reaffirm a doctrine of incarnation. It will have to learn to appropriate for itself a narrative of the following form:

In the beginning was the Word,
and the Word was with God,
and the Word was God . . .
Through him all things were made . . .
In him was life, and that life was the light of all people . . .
The Word became flesh and made his dwelling among us.

CONCLUSION

In the preface of this book I compared its methodology to that of a hostess at a dinner party who is required to introduce a late arrival to a number of her distinguished guests. She offers a summary of the preceding conversation so that the newcomer might be able to understand what has been going on and possibly participate in the discussion as it develops. At some stage in the evening a number of the younger guests move into an adjoining room, continuing the same topic of conversation but taking it in quite new directions. They often break up into even smaller groups as they pursue their particular lines of thought. Mixing with her guests the hostess becomes aware that there is a growing interest among some of these newer circles to re-engage with the original conversation. But they are not sure how they can do so with integrity.

This final chapter is no more than a suggested set of parameters for that corporate discussion.

NOTES

CHAPTER 1: THE PARADOX

[1] The Koran indicates that to confuse creator and creature constitutes the unforgivable sin. 'God forgives not that aught should be with him associated (4.48)'

[2] See C. F. D. Moule, *The Origin of Christology* (Cambridge, Cambridge University Press, 1977); James D. G. Dunn, *Christology in the Making: An Inquiry into the Origins of the Doctrine of the Incarnation* (London, SCM Press, 1980)

[3] Larry W. Hurtado, *How on Earth Did Jesus Become a God? Historical Questions about Earliest Devotion to Jesus* (Grand Rapids, Michigan, William B. Eerdmans Publishing Company, 2005) p. 25. See also Richard Baukham, *God Crucified: Monotheism and Christology in the New Testament* (Carlisle, Paternoster Press, 1998)

[4] Phil. 2.5–11

[5] Karl Rahner, *Theological Investigations*, vol. IV, E. T. by Kevin Smyth (London, Darton, Longman and Todd, 1966) p. 105

CHAPTER 2: INCARNATION

[6] Irenaeus, *Against Heresies* IV 6.7, ANF vol. I, p. 469

[7] Charles Bigg, *Christian Platonists of Alexandria* (Oxford, 1886) reprinted by Kessinger Publishing, 2003, p. 28. Quoted in the article on 'Gnosticism' in *A New Dictionary of Christian Theology* ed. by Alan Richardson and John Bowden (London, SCM Press, 1985) p. 227

CHAPTER 4: THE HUMAN MIND OF THE WORD GOD

[8] J. N. D. Kelly, *Early Christian Doctrines*, fifth edition (London, Adam and Charles Black, 1977) pp. 285–286

[9] Athanasius, *Four Discourses Against the Arians*, III 34, NPNF, second series, vol. IV, p. 412

[10] Ibid., III 35, p. 413

[11] Ibid., III 51, pp. 421–422

[12] See R. V. Sellers, *Two Ancient Christologies: A Study in the Christological Thought of the Schools of Alexandria and Antioch in the Early History of Christian Doctrine* (London, SPCK, 1954) p. 137

[13] *Early Christian Doctrines*, p. 305

[14] Quoted in *Early Christian Doctrines*, p. 305

[15] *Early Christian Doctrines*, p. 307

[16] The Symbol of Union or Formula of Union was a creed drafted by the Oriental or Antiochene party who arrived too late to participate in the decisions of the Council of Ephesus 431, the Third General Council of the Church. The Symbol formed the bulk of Cyril of Alexandria's letter to John of Antioch and helped to restore communion between the rival Alexandrian and Antiochene parties. It paved the way for the Chalcedonian settlement some 20 years later

CHAPTER 5: DIVINE AND HUMAN WILLING IN CHRIST

[17] See R.V. Sellers, *Two Ancient Christologies: A Study in the Christological Thought of the Schools of Alexandria and Antioch in the Early History of Christian Doctrine* (London, SPCK, 1954) p. 202

[18] Aloys Grillmeier, *Christ in Christian Tradition*, vol. 2, translated by John Cawte (Atlanta, John Knox Press, 1986) p. 109

CHAPTER 6: JESUS AND THE SPIRIT

[19] *Against Heresies*, 3.9.3, p. 423

[20] Ibid., III 17.3, p. 445. The key to this interpretation is the realization that by 'his own man' Irenaeus refers to Christ's human nature. Kelly draws attention to Irenaeus' lack of an abstract term for humanity. p. 148

[21] Theodore of Mopsuestia, quoted in R. A. Norris, *Manhood and Christ: A Study in the Christology of Theodore of Mopsuestia* (Oxford, Clarendon Press, 1963) p. 204

[22] H. B. Swete, *The Holy Spirit in the Ancient Church* (London, Epworth Press, 1912) p. 260

[23] Ibid., p. 80

[24] *Manhood and Christ*, p. 214.

[25] R. L. Ottley, *The Doctrine of the Incarnation* (London, Methuen & Co. Ltd., 1911) p. 464

[26] John Owen, *On the Person of Christ*, Works I (ed.) William H. Goold (London, The Banner of Truth, Trust, 1966) pp. 170–171

[27] John Owen, *An Exposition of the Epistle to the Hebrews* (Grand Rapids, Michigan, Baker House, 1980), p. 422

[28] *On the Person of Christ*, Works I, p. 326

[29] John Owen, *On the Person of Christ*, Works II (ed.) William H. Goold (London, The Banner of Truth, Trust, 1966) pp. 414–415

[30] John Owen, *Pneumatalogia: Or, A Discourse Concerning the Holy Spirit*, Works 3 (ed.) William H. Goold (London, The Banner of Truth, Trust, 1966) pp. 160–161

CHAPTER 7: THE SOCINIAN CHALLENGE TO NICEA

[31] *Racovian Catechism*, E. T. from the Latin by Thomas Rees (London, Longman, Rees, Orme and Brown Paternoster Row, 1818)
[32] The Socinians were notable textual critics
[33] J. Toland, *Christianity not Mysterious*, 1696; J. Locke, *Reasonableness of Christianity*, 1695

CHAPTER 8: IN SEARCH OF THE HISTORICAL JESUS

[34] See Colin Gunton, *Enlightenment and Alienation: An Essay towards a Trinitarian Theology* (Marshall, Morgan & Scott, 1985) p. 4

CHAPTER 9: A THEOLOGY OF RELIGIOUS EXPERIENCE

[35] Quoted by P. T. Forsyth in *The Person and Place of Jesus Christ* (London, United Reformed Church, 1999) p. 220

CHAPTER 10: THE CHRIST OF FAITH AND THE JESUS OF HISTORY

[36] Quoted by James F. Kay in *Christus Praesens: Reconsideration of Rudolph Bultmann's Christology* (Grand Rapids, Michigan, William B. Eerdmans Publishing Co., 1994) note 26, p. 44
[37] Quoted by Gareth Jones in *Bultmann: Towards a Critical Theology* (Cambridge, Polity Press, 1991) p. 16

CHAPTER 11: THE DOCTRINE OF WORD OF GOD

[38] See John Webster, *Karl Barth* (second edition) (London and New York, Continuum, 2004), p. 52
[39] Wolfhart Pannenburg, *Jesus – God and Man* (London, SCM Press, 1985) p. 406

CHAPTER 12: RESURRECTION AS REVELATION

[40] Wolfhart Pannenburg, *Jesus – God and Man* (London, SCM Press, 1985) p. 29

CHAPTER 13: AN ECUMENICAL CHRISTOLOY

[41] The active humanity of Christ has played a significant role in soteriological thought throughout the tradition, as it has in the Scriptures. See Alan Spence, *The Promise of Peace: A Unified Theory of the Atonement* (London, T&T Clark, 2006) Chapter Two

[42] Such coherence was, as we have indicated, ably demonstrated not only in the post-Chalcedonian discussion but also by the Puritan John Owen in his exposition of the work of the Holy Spirit in the person of Jesus, see Alan Spence, *Incarnation and Inspiration: John Owen and the Coherence of Christology* (London, T&T Clark, 2007)

[43] Trevor Hart makes a helpful observation on the use of the concept of *hypostasis* with respect to the humanity of Christ. 'Since *hypostasis* is a transcendental category rather than a predicate there is nothing of God's nature present phenomenally.' Trevor Hart, 'Revelation' in *The Cambridge Companion to Karl Barth*, ed. by John Webster (Cambridge, Cambridge University Press, 2000) p. 52

SELECTED BIBLIOGRAPHY

Athanasius, *De Synodis*, Nicene and Post-Nicene Fathers, second series, vol. 4, reprinted by William B Eerdmans (Grand Rapids, Michigan, 1980) p. 457

—*Four Discourses Against the Arians*, NPNF, second series, vol. IV, William B. Eerdmans Publishing Company (Grand Rapids, Michigan, 1980)

—*On the Incarnation*, NPNF, second series, vol. IV, Grand Rapids, William B Eerdmans Publishing Company (Grand Rapids, Michigan, 1980)

Baillie, D. M., *God was in Christ: An Essay on Incarnation and Atonement* (London, Faber & Faber Limited, 1961)

Barth, Karl, *Church Dogmatics*, E. T. G. W. Bromiley (Edinburgh, T&T Clark, 1985)

Baukham, Richard, *God Crucified: Monotheism and Christology in the New Testament* (Carlisle, Paternoster Press, 1998)

Bettenson, Henry (ed.), *Documents of the Christian Church* (New York, Oxford University Press, 1967) pp. 51–52

Bigg, Charles, *Christian Platonists of Alexandria* (Oxford, 1886) reprinted by Kessinger Publishing, 2003

Bornkamm, Günther, *Jesus of Nazareth* (London, Hodder and Stoughton, 1973)

Bultmann, Rudolph, *Theology of the New Testament*, vol. 1, E. T. Kendrick Grobel (London, SCM Press, 1965)

—*New Testament and Mythology and Other Basic Writings* (ed.) Schubert M. Ogden (Augsburg Fortress, 1990)

Creeds, Councils and Controversies, Documents Illustrative of the History of the Church A.D. 337–461, edited by J. Stevenson (London, 1966) p. 101.

Crisp, Oliver D., *Divinity and Humanity* (Cambridge, Cambridge University Press, 2007)

Cyril of Alexandria, *Third Letter to Nestorius, Cyril of Alexandria: Select Letters*, Ed. and E. T. Lionel R. Wickam (Oxford, Clarendon Press, 1983)

Dunn, James D. G., *Christology in the Making: An Inquiry into the Origins of the Doctrine of the Incarnation* (London, SCM Press, 1980)

Epiphanius of Salamis, *Panarion* 30.16.4–5, in *The Apocryphal New Testament*, translated by Montague Rhode James (Oxford, 1924), p. 10

Forsyth, P. T., *The Person and Place of Jesus Christ* (London, United Reformed Church, 1999)

Gregg, Robert C. and Dennis E. Groh, *Early Arianism: A View of Salvation* (London, SCM Press Ltd., 1981)

Gregory Nazianzen, *To Cledonius the Priest against Apollinarius*, NPNF, second series, vol. VII

Grillmeier, Aloys, *Christ in Christian Tradition*, vol. 1, E. T. John Bowden (London and Oxford, Mowbrays, 1975)

—*Christ in Christian Tradition*, vol. 2, translated John Cawte (Atlanta, John Knox Press, 1986)

Gunton, Colin, *Enlightenment and Alienation: An Essay towards a Trinitarian Theology* (Marshall, Morgan & Scott, 1985)

Hunsinger, George, *Disruptive Grace: Studies in the Theology of Karl Barth* (Grand Rapids, Michigan/Cambridge UK, William B Eerdmans Publishing Company, 2000)

Hurtado, Larry W., *How on Earth Did Jesus Become a God? Historical Questions about Earliest Devotion to Jesus* (Grand Rapids, Michigan, William B Eerdmans Publishing Company, 2005)

Ignatius, *Epistle to the Ephesians*, Ante-Nicene Fathers, vol. 1, reprinted by William B Eerdmans (Grand Rapids, Michigan, 1985)

—*Epistle to the Smyrnaens 2*, Ante-Nicene Fathers, vol. 1, reprinted by William B Eerdmans (Grand Rapids, Michigan, 1985) p. 87

—*Epistle to the Trallians 9*, Ante-Nicene Fathers, vol. 1, reprinted by William B Eerdmans (Grand Rapids, Michigan, 1985) p. 70

Irenaeus, *Against Heresies*, Ante-Nicene Fathers, vol. 1, reprinted by William B Eerdmans (Grand Rapids, Michigan, 1985)

—*Against Heresies*, ANF, vol. 2, reprinted by William B Eerdmans (Grand Rapids, Michigan, 1985)

John of Damascus, *Exposition of the Orthodox Faith*, The Nicene and Post-Nicene Fathers, second series, vol. 9, reprinted by William B Eerdmans (Grand Rapids, Michigan, 1976) 3.15, p. 60

Jones, Gareth, *Bultmann: Towards a Critical Theology* (Cambridge, Polity Press, 1991)

Justin Martyr, *Apology*, ANF, vol. I, William B Eerdmans Publishing Company (Grand Rapids, Michigan, 1985)

—*Dialogue with Trypho*, Ante-Nicene Fathers, vol. 1, reprinted by William B Eerdmans (Grand Rapids, Michigan, 1985)

Kähler, Martin, *The So-called Historical Jesus and the Historic Biblical Christ*, E. T. Caarl E. Braaten (Philadelphia, Fortress Press, 1964)

Kay, James F., *Christus Praesens: Reconsideration of Rudolph Bultmann's Christology* (Grand Rapids, Michigan, William B Eerdmans Publishing Co., 1994)

Kelly, J. N. D., *Early Christian Creeds*, third edition (Longman, 1972)

—*Early Christian Doctrines*, fifth edition (London, Adam & Charles Black, 1977)

Kung, Hans, *The Incarnation of God*, E. T. J. R. Stevenson (Edinburgh, T&T. Clark, 1987)

Leo, 'The Tome of Leo' in *Creeds, Councils and Controversies* (ed.) J. Stevenson (London, SPCK, 1966)

Locke, John, *Reasonableness of Christianity* (Oxford, Regnery Publishing, 1998)

MacKinnon, D. M., '"Substance" in Christology – a cross-bench view' in *Christ Faith and History*, Cambridge Studies in Christology (ed.) S. W. Sykes and J. P. Clayton (Cambridge, Cambridge University Press, 1978)

McCready, Douglas, *He Came Down from Heaven* (Downers Grove, Illinois, InterVarsity Press, 2005)

McLachlan, H. John, *Socinianism in Seventeenth-century England* (Oxford, Oxford University Press, 1951)

Moule, C. F. D., *The Origin of Christology* (Cambridge, Cambridge University Press, 1977)

Norris, R. A., *Manhood and Christ: A Study in the Christology of Theodore of Mopsuestia* (Oxford, Clarendon Press, 1963)

Ottley, R. L., *The Doctrine of the Incarnation* (London, Methuen & Co. Ltd., 1911)

Owen, John, *An Exposition of the Epistle to the Hebrews* (Grand Rapids, Michigan, Baker House, 1980)

—*On the Person of Christ*, Works I (ed.) William H. Goold (London, The Banner of Truth, Trust, 1966)

—*On the Person of Christ*, Works II (ed.) by William H. Goold (London, The Banner of Truth, Trust, 1966) pp. 414–415

—*Pneumatalogia: Or, A Discourse concerning the Holy Spirit*, Works 3 (ed.) William H. Goold (London, The Banner of Truth, Trust, 1966)

Pannenberg, Wolfhart, *Jesus – God and Man* (London, SCM Press, 1985)

Racovian Catechism, E. T. from the Latin by Thomas Rees (London, Longman, Rees, Orme and Brown Paternoster Row, 1818)

Rahner, Karl, *Theological Investigations,* vol. IV, E. T. Kevin Smyth (London, Darton, Longman & Todd, 1966)

Reimarus, Herman Samuel, 'On the Intention of Jesus' in *Reimarus: Fragments*, E. T. Charles H. Talbert (1971)

Relton, Maurice, *A Study in Christology, The Problem of the Relation of the Two Natures in the Person of Christ* (London, SPCK, 1934) (New York, The Macmillan Company)

Schillebeeckx, E., *Jesus: An Experiment in Christology* (London, Fount Paperbacks, 1983)

Schleiermacher, Fredrich, *The Christian Faith* (Edinburgh, T&T Clark, 1976)

Schweitzer, Albert, *The Quest of the Historical Jesus: A Critical Study of its Progress from Reimarus to Wrede* (London, SCM Press Ltd., 1954)

Sellers, R. V., *Two Ancient Christologies: A Study in the Christological Thought of the Schools of Alexandria and Antioch in the Early History of Christian Doctrine* (London, SPCK, 1954)

Spence, Alan J., *Incarnation and Inspiration: John Owen and the Coherence of Christology* (T&T Clark, London, 2007)

—*The Promise of Peace: A Unified Theory of Atonement* (T&T Clark, London, 2006)

Stead, Christopher, *Divine Substance* (Oxford, Clarendon Press, 1977)

Swete, H. B., *The Holy Spirit in the Ancient Church* (London, Epworth Press, 1912)

Theodoret, *Cyril's 'Twelve Chapters' or Anathemas with Theodoret's Counter-Statements*, NPNF, second series, vol. III

Toland, J., *Christianity not Mysterious* (London, Sam Buckley, 1696)

Waldrop, Charles T., *Karl Barth's Christology: Its Basic Alexandrian Character* (Mouton Publishers, 1984)

Warfield, Benjamin B., *John Calvin the Theologian* (Presbyterian Board of Education 1909) http://homepage.mac.com/shanerosenthal/reformationink/bbwcalvin1.htm, accessed on 7 April 2008

Webster, John, *Karl Barth*, second edition (London, New York, Continuum, 2004)

Webster, John (ed.) *The Cambridge Companion to Karl Barth* (Cambridge, Cambridge University Press, 2000)

Works of Dionysius the Areopagite, The, translated by John Parker (London and Oxford, 1897), p. 143

Young, Frances, *From Nicea to Chalcedon: A Guide to the Literature and Its Background* (London, SCM Press Ltd., 1983)

INDEX